Alexander Balloch Grosart, Philip Sidney

The Complete Poems of Sir Philip Sidney

Vol. I

Alexander Balloch Grosart, Philip Sidney

The Complete Poems of Sir Philip Sidney
Vol. I

ISBN/EAN: 9783744687782

Printed in Europe, USA, Canada, Australia, Japan

Cover: Foto ©Thomas Meinert / pixelio.de

More available books at **www.hansebooks.com**

Early English Poets.

THE
COMPLETE POEMS

OF

SIR PHILIP SIDNEY.

EDITED,

WITH

Memorial-Introduction and Notes,

BY THE

REV. ALEXANDER B. GROSART.

IN THREE VOLUMES.—VOL. I.

London:
CHATTO AND WINDUS, PICCADILLY.
1877.

TO

DAVID MASSON, ESQ. M.A. LL.D.

PROFESSOR OF RHETORIC AND ENGLISH LITERATURE IN THE
UNIVERSITY OF EDINBURGH,
AUTHOR OF THE LIFE OF JOHN MILTON,
NARRATED IN CONNECTION WITH THE POLITICAL, ECCLESIASTICAL, AND
LITERARY HISTORY OF HIS TIME, ETC.

I Dedicate

THIS THE FIRST COMPLETE EDITION OF THE POETRY OF

SIR PHILIP SIDNEY,

ASSURED THAT MY 'LABOUR OF LOVE' WILL BE

SYMPATHETICALLY REGARDED BY HIM,

AND AS A 'PEPPER-CORN' ACKNOWLEDGMENT

OF OBLIGATIONS WHILE PURSUING RESEARCHES KINDRED

WITH HIS OWN IN 'MILTON.'

I LIKE TOO TO RE-LINK MYSELF THUS WITH MY

ALMA MATER AND AN OLD CLASS-ROOM.

VERY FAITHFULLY AND GRATEFULLY,

ALEXANDER B. GROSART.

Preface.

PERHAPS it will generally be admitted that it is one of the most inexplicable of the many 'Curiosities' and anomalies of our Literature, that ours should be, to all intents and purposes, the first collective edition, as it is absolutely the first critical text, of the Poems of SIR PHILIP SIDNEY. Following the Trade edition of the Works (3 vols. 12mo, 1739), Gray, in his 'Miscellaneous Works' of Sidney (Oxford, 1829: Boston, 1860, 8vo), satisfied himself with 'Astrophel and Stella,' and 'Certaine Sonnets' and other Poems, which he placed under the heading 'Miscellaneous Poems,'—utterly ignoring the much more numerous Poems contained in the 'Arcadia' and 'Psalmes.' He added from Dr. Bliss's edition of the Athenæ Oxon. and Bibliog. Miscellanies, and elsewhere, slightly. There is no other available edition. So that it must surely be regarded as a desideratum worth supplying, to reproduce, as we herein do, the complete Poems of Sidney.

In an Essay in the present Volume we discuss

such points in this remarkable poetry as in our judgment called for discussion. Thither we refer the Reader.

I have only here the pleasant duty of acknowledging my sense of obligation to the noble present owners of Penshurst and Wilton for their kind facilities in relation to their Sidney treasures. Alas! that a fire within recent years swept away all the Manuscripts of Sidney preserved at Wilton, save the Lines to Elizabeth, along with a lock of her hair,—sunny as gold, and 'red' only as gold was used to be called red! Penshurst, with abundant Sidney documents, proved to hold nothing poetical except John Davies of Hereford's transcript of the Psalms,—acquired at the Bright sale for 4*l.* 16*s.*, as I learn from a priced catalogue.

To the EARL OF WARWICK AND BROOKE I am indebted for the long loan to my Engraver (Mr. W. J. Alais) of his priceless original Portrait, formerly in the possession of Fulke Greville, Lord Brooke. It seems to me a very noble Portrait, and self-authenticating in every way. The original is somewhat faded, touched with ' Decay's effacing fingers.' It has never before been engraved. As now presented, it must surely be pronounced *the* Portrait of Sir Philip Sidney, being 'sweet,' after the deep old meaning of that word, and yet mind-full, gracious in its aspect, but sheathing power; soft and tender about the mouth, nevertheless carrying mobilities of swift passion—as the tranquil sea its fierceness and strength; and above all, realising to us the many-storied steep forehead (like Scott's), telling of a sovran soul within. I cannot sufficiently acknowledge the kindness of the noble owner in permitting me the use of it,—as before of Fulke Greville, Lord Brooke's MSS. To the most noble the MARQUIS OF SALISBURY I wish to return my heartfelt thanks for the Lady Rich Letters, herein first printed,—part of very many other precious discoveries made while at Hatfield, of which more again.

In the Notes and Illustrations, and in the preparation of the text throughout, I have again emphatically to acknowledge infinite obligation to my unfailing friend Dr. BRINSLEY NICHOLSON: anything finer than his devoted perseverance throughout in consulting all possible authorities to aid me, I know not. Alas! that as I write these words my beloved friend is laid on a perilous sick-bed. I have also to thank right cordially W. ALDIS WRIGHT, Esq., M.A., Trinity College, Cambridge, for a collation of the Trinity-College

MS. of the 'Psalmes'; and the authorities of the Bodleian and British Museum for their invariable helpfulness. I wish also to express my indebtedness to S. CHRISTIE-MILLER, Esq., Britwell, for his pleasant communications on books and MSS. in his incomparable Collections.

Our Essay and Notes and Illustrations give all else necessary. In conclusion here, I commend the view enunciated by me of the Astrophel and Stella Sonnets and Songs, and 'Sidera,' to the consideration of any who may have been wont to look upon them as mere literary exercises or pastimes. To my mind, such a conception of them misses the deepest, the most intense, the (in a sense) most awful chapter in Sir Philip Sidney's life-story; for it is my conviction that never was love (ultimately) more impassioned, or anguish more keen, or moral struggle more agitating, or final victory more absolute, than in Sidney and Stella, and in Stella equally with Sidney.

In publishing my erewhile private edition of Sidney, it may be stated that throughout the text has been re-collated, and the notes and illustrations carefully revised and corrected. Herein I wish heartily to acknowledge the kind interest and helpfulness of my two excellent literary friends, J. M. THOMSON, Esq., Charlotte Square, Edinburgh, and G. H. WHITE, Esq., Torquay, Devonshire.

ALEXANDER B. GROSART.

St. George's, Blackburn, Lancashire.

Contents.

	PAGE
DEDICATION	v
PREFACE	vii
ESSAY ON THE POETRY OF SIDNEY	xxi
I. ASTROPHEL AND STELLA :—	
NOTE	3
I. Looke in thy heart, and write	5
II. Love gave the wound	6
III. All my deed but copying is	8
IV. Vertue, thou thy selfe shalt be in loue	10
V. True beautie vertue is	11
VI. I do Stella love	12
VII. Stella's eyes in colour black	13
VIII. Love . . . in my close heart	15
IX. Vertue's Court	16
X. Reason and Loue	18
XI. Love, thou leav'st the best behinde	20
XII. Cupid	20
XIII. Phœbus	22
XIV. Alas, haue I not paine enough	23
XV. Dictionarie's methode	24
XVI. Loue's pain	25
XVII. Cupid offending	27
XVIII. Bankrout	28
XIX. Words . . . vainely spent	29
XX. My death's wound	30

CONTENTS.

ASTROPHEL AND STELLA *(continued)*

	PAGE
XXI. Aught so faire as Stella is	31
XXII. The Sunne . . . did her but kisse	33
XXIII. Pensivenesse	34
XXIV. Rich, more wretched	36
XXV. Vertue . . . takes Stella's shape	37
XXVI. Astrologie	39
XXVII. Most alone in greatest company	40
XXVIII. Allegorie	41
XXIX. Given vp for a slaue	42
XXX. Questions	44
XXXI. The Moone	45
XXXII. Morpheus	48
XXXIII. I might	49
XXXIV. How can words ease	50
XXXV. Grow rich, meaning my Stella's name	51
XXXVI. New assaults	53
XXXVII. No misfortune but that Rich she is	54
XXXVIII. The unkinde guest	55
XXXIX. Sleepe	57
XL. Nowe of the basest	58
XLI. Stella lookt on	60
XLII. Eyes	61
XLIII. Leaue to die	62
XLIV. Inward smart	63
XLV. Imag'd things	64
XLVI. Blind-hitting Boy	65
XLVII. Gaine to misse	66
XLVIII. Sweete cruell shot	67
XLIX. I on my horse	68

CONTENTS.

ASTROPHEL AND STELLA *(continued)*

		PAGE
L.	Fulnesse of thoughts	69
LI.	Pardon mine cares	70
LII.	Vertue and Loue	71
LIII.	What now, Sir Foole	72
LIV.	They love indeed who quake to say they love	74
LV.	Muses . . . holy ayde	75
LVI.	Patience	76
LVII.	My paines me reioyce	77
LVIII.	Soueraignty	78
LIX.	More of a dog then me	80
LX.	Blest in my curse	81
LXI.	Angel's sophistrie	82
LXII.	Watred was my wine	83
LXIII.	No, no	84
LXIV.	Do not will me from my loue to flie	85
LXV.	Loue . . . vnkind	86
LXVI.	Hope to feede	88
LXVII.	More truth, more paine	89
LXVIII.	Planet of my light	90
LXIX.	Couenant	91
LXX.	Wise silence	92
LXXI.	Inward sunne	93
LXXII.	My onely Deare	95
LXXIII.	Kisse	96
LXXIV.	I am no pickpurse of another's wit	97
LXXV.	Edward IV.	98
LXXVI.	Gentle force	99
LXXVII.	A meane price	101

CONTENTS.

ASTROPHEL AND STELLA *(continued)*

		PAGE
LXXVIII.	Ielousie	102
LXXIX.	Sweetnesse	103
LXXX.	Sweet lipp	105
LXXXI.	Still, still, kiss	107
LXXXII.	Cherries	108
LXXXIII.	To a Sparrow	109
LXXXIV.	My Muse	111
LXXXV.	Kingly tribute	112
LXXXVI.	Sweet Iudge	113
LXXXVII.	Duetie to depart	114
LXXXVIII.	Absence	115
LXXXIX.	Day and Night	116
XC.	Fame	117
XCI.	You in them I love	118
XCII.	All said, still say the same	119
XCIII.	Tho' worlds 'quite me, shall I my selfe forgiue	121
XCIV.	Griefe	122
XCV.	Sighes	123
XCVI.	Thought	125
XCVII.	Dian's peere	127
XCVIII.	Loue's Spur	128
XCIX.	Sleep's Armory	129
C.	All mirth farewell	132
CI.	Stella is sicke	133
CII.	It is but loue	135
CIII.	Golden Haire	137
CIV.	Enuious wits	138
CV.	Unhappie	140

ASTROPHEL AND STELLA *(continued)*

 cvi. Absent presence 142
 cvii. See what it is to loue 143
 cviii. Rude Despaire 144
 cix. Desire 146
 cx. Aspire to higher things 147

SONGS IN ASTROPHEL AND STELLA:—

 First Song 151
 Second Song 155
 Third Song 157
 Fourth Song 159
 Fift Song 163
 Sixt Song 173
 Seuenth Song 176
 Eight Song 179
 Ninth Song 187
 Tenth Song 190
 Eleuenth Song 193

ESSAY ON THE POETRY OF SIR PHILIP SIDNEY,

BEING A

MEMORIAL-INTRODUCTION.

Memorial-Introduction.

ESSAY ON THE POETRY OF SIR PHILIP SIDNEY.

Born at Penshurst, Kent, 1554: died, after Battle of Zutphen, 1586.

WHILE besides earlier and later there have been no fewer than three considerable recent Lives of Sir Philip Sidney, viz. by Bourne,[1] Lloyd,[2] and an anonymous American,[3] it must be stated that *the* Life —such as should take its place inevitably with dear old Izaak Walton's 'Lives,' or Southey's 'Nelson '— remains unwritten. This is our judgment, after a prolonged and careful study of all the Sidney-literature. We shall indulge the 'pleasures of hope' that one day such a biography of this great Englishman will appear; for there are lights and shadows, heights and depths—

[1] A Memoir of Sir Philip Sidney. By H. R. Fox Bourne. 1 vol. 8vo, 1862 (Chapman and Hall), pp. xv. and 557.
[2] The Life of Sir Philip Sidney. By Julius Lloyd, M.A. 1862 (Longman), pp. xvi. and 244.
[3] The Life and Times of Sir Philip Sidney. Boston (Ticknor), 1859: pp. 281: recently re-issued in daintier form.

ay, depths—in that Life, that have thus far been only very imperfectly sounded.

It were out of proportion for an Editor of his Poems simply, to retraverse the Facts and Teachings of the full Biography. But there are certain things in relation to the Poems, which may be considered acceptably, as a contribution to the ultimate Life, and as a fitting introduction to this first-complete, critical, and adequately annotated collection of these Poems. The incompleteness of all editions hitherto lies on the surface, inasmuch as the amount of ours is increased by more than a half compared with Gray's (Oxford, 1829), and its American reprint (Boston, 1860), or any other so-called collective edition of Sidney's Poetry; while our Notes and Illustrations reveal a literary chaos in the text. We propose to consider the following points in this Essay:

I. The original and after-editions of the successive sets of Poems as herein reproduced.

II. The texts of our edition, punctuation and line-arrangement, classification, &c.

III. The story of Lady Rich and Sidney in the *morale* of it, with hitherto unprinted letters.

IV. The characteristics of Sidney's Poetry, with the praises of it by his contemporaries and onward. These in order.

MEMORIAL-INTRODUCTION. xxiii

1. *The original and after editions of the successive Poems as herein reproduced.*

The entire Writings of Sidney, Prose and Verse, were posthumously printed. He was known and even 'renowned' for his Poetry and Prose during his life time, but wholly through manuscript copies put into circulation, as was the *mode*, by himself and friends.

His 'Arcadia'—which contains so large a portion of his Verse—was 'designed' to be published immediately after his death in 1586, and it was his first appearance from the press, but this was not until 1590 : 'The Covntesse of Pembrokes Arcadia, written by Sir Philippe Sidnei: London, Printed for William Ponsonbie, Anno Domini 1590' (4to.) A copy is in the British Museum. A letter preserved in the State-Paper Office from Fulke Greville, Lord Brooke, to Sidney's father-in-law Sir Francis Walsingham, is indorsed 'November, 1586'; and as it sheds light on various points to be afterwards noticed, must be here given, as follows :

'To the Right honorable S^r francis Walsingham.
'S^r, this day, one ponsonby, a booke-bynder in poles church yard, came to me and told me that ther was one in hand to print Sr Philip Sydney's old arcadia, asking me

yf it were done with your honors consent, or any other of his frendes? I told him, to my knowledge, no: then he advysed me to give warninge of it, either to the archbishope or doctor Cosen, who have, as he says, a copy to peruse to that end.

'S^r, I am loth to renew his memory unto you, but yeat in this I must presume; for I have sent my lady, your daughter, at her request, a correction of that old one, don 4 or 5 years sinse, which he left in trust with me; wherof there is no more copies, and fitter to be printed then the first, which is so common : notwithstanding, even that to be amended by a direction sett downe undre his own hand, how and why; so as in many respects, espetially the care of printing of it, is to be don with more deliberation.

' Besydes, he hathe most excellently translated, among divers other notable workes, monsieur du Plessis book against Atheisme, which is sinse don by an other; so as both in respect of lov between Plessis and him, besydes other affinities in ther courses, but espetially Sr Philip's uncomparable judgement, I think fit ther be made stay of that mercenary book, so that Sr Philip might have all thos religious works which ar worthily dew to his lyfe and death.

' Many other works, as Bartas his Spanyard, 40 of the psalms translated into myter, &c. which requyre the care of his frends, not to amend, for I think it falls within the reach of no man living, but only to see to the paper, and other common errors of mercenary printing. Gayn ther wilbe, no doubt, to be disposed by you: let it be to the poorest of his servants; I desyre only care to be had of

MEMORIAL-INTRODUCTION. xxv

his honor, who, I fear, hath caried the honor of thes latter ages with him.

'S^r, pardon me, I make this the busines of my lofe [=love], and desyre God to shew that he is your God. From my Lodge, not well, this day in hast. Your honors

'FOULK GREVILL.

'S^r, I had wayted on you my selfe for answer, because I am jelous of tyme in it, but in trothe I am nothing well. Good S^r, think of it.'⁴

It is to be observed that the 'Ponsonby' named by Lord Brooke was the Publisher of the 'Arcadia' of 1590 (4to), as he was likewise of the folios of 1593, 1598, and later. In 1588, '23 Augusti,' he had entered 'Arcadia' for the press, as appears from the following entry in the Stationers' Registers:

'Wm. Ponsonby. Rd. of him for a booke of Sr Php. Sidney's makinge, intitled Arcadia : authorised under the Archb. of Cante. hand . . . vj^{d'} ⁵

'The 'Arcadia' of 1590 is defective in many ways, as an examination of a copy in the British Museum has shown us; but it was not until 1593 that another and more accurate edition appeared. To it was pre-

---

⁴ J. Payne Collier's Life of Spenser (Works, vol. i. pp. liii. iv.); also in his Bib. Catalogue under 'Sydney.' I have bracketed 'love' instead of 'life' of Mr. Collier's, as more probably Lord Brooke's word.   ⁵ Collier, as before, p. liv.

fixed a notable Epistle signed 'H. S.,'[6] pointing out the errors of the former, and claiming for the new all authority. Who 'H. S.' was has never been discovered. The 'S.' suggests one of the family; but the 'H.' perplexes. From 1590 to 1725 the 'Arcadia' was a 'quick' book in successive (folio) editions. Of certain of these, more in the sequel.

'Astrophel and Stella' was first published in 1591. There were three editions of this year. The first, which has been designated 'surreptitious,'[7] bears this title-page:

'Syr P. S. his Astrophel and Stella. Wherein the excellence of Sweete Poesie is concluded. To the end of which are added sundry other rare Sonnets of diuers Noblemen and Gentlemen. At London, Printed for Thomas Newman, Anno Domini 1591' (4to).

A second edition of 1591 has this title-page:

'Sir P. S. his Astrophel and Stella. Wherein the excellence of Sweete Poesie is concluded. At London, Printed for Thomas Newman, 1591.'

The former contains forty-four leaves, this thirty-

---

[6] See the Epistle *in extenso* at close of our Notes and Illustrations to 'Astrophel and Stella,' &c. in vol. iii.

[7] By Mr. Collier, as before, p. cxv. and Bib. Catalogue, *s.n.*

MEMORIAL-INTRODUCTION. xxvii

two leaves only; the latter omitting the 'sundry other rare Sonnets,' and the Epistles of the Publisher and Thomas Nash. A third edition, 'At London, Printed for Matthew Lownes,' corresponds with the first. A copy is in the Bodleian (Malone), and is without date; but another copy, at Britwell,[8] is dated, like the others, 1591; not 1595, the date assigned to it by Mr. Hazlitt (Bibliography of Old English Literature, *s. n.*). Of the relative authority of these editions I shall hereafter speak.

The 'Arcadia' of 1598 first published the set of Poems that in all the after folios appeared as 'Certaine Sonets Written by Sir Philip Sidney. Neuer before printed.' Of these onward.

The 'Apologie for Poetrie' appeared originally in 1595. 'At London, Printed for Henry Olney, and are to be sold at his shop in Paule's Churchyard, at the signe of the George, neere to Cheap-gate.' It was of this 'Apologie'—later named 'Defence'—William Cowper was thinking when he finely sang of Sidney as 'warbler of poetic prose'; but as it does not con-

---

[8] I owe special thanks to S. Christie-Miller, Esq., for his many painstaking communications to me on his Sidney and other treasures.

tain any of his verse, it falls not to be noticed further by us.[9]

The 'Psalmes' in 'myter' remained in manuscript until so recently as 1823. Of these and our text of Sidney's portion I speak fully in the relative introductory Note.

The minor pieces, which we have arranged under the heading of 'Pansies from Penshurst and Wilton,' appeared in Davison's 'Poetical Rhapsody' (1602) and other collections, as pointed out in their places.[1]

The translations from Du Bartas seem to have perished. That they existed is clear, not only from

---

[9] Had not the 'Defense of Poetrie' been admirably reprinted by Mr. Arber, we should certainly have included it in our edition of the Poems, instinct as it is with poetry. Now it were superfluous, seeing it is to be had for a mere trifle, as well as the related books of Stubbes and Gosson.

[1] The reprints of Davison give full details of the different authors. Looking beyond Davison, it may be noted that Puttenham in his 'Art of Poesie' quotes Sidney, e.g. last two lines of 'To the tune of a Neapolitan Villanel' (p. 212, Arber's reprint); the ditty in full, Arcadia, B iii. p. 352 (1613) (p. 233, ibid.); and the last two lines of quatorzain in Arcadia, B iii. p. 283:

> What medcine then . . .
> Where loue . . .

(p. 225, ibid). So too in England's Parnassus there are various passages from Arcadia and Astrophel and Stella.

Lord Brooke's mention of them, but also from Ponsonby's entry in the Stationers' Register, thus, under same date with the 'Arcadia' (23d Aug. 1588):

Wm. Ponsonby. Item, Rd. of him for a translation of Salust de Bartas, done by the same Sr P. into englishe . . . . . . vj^d'

Florio, too, in the dedication of the Second Book of his translation of Montaigne (fol. 1603), tells Lady Rutland and Lady Penelope Rich that he had ' seene the first septimaine of that arch-poet Du Bartas' rendered into English by Sidney, and he entreats them to honour the age by making it public. In relation to this, a friend calls my attention to Du Bartas, Premier Jour de la première Sepmaine, ll. 155-160:

"Mais, tous tels que l'enfant, qui se paist das l'eschole,
Pour l'estude des arts, d'un estude frivole,
Nostre veil admire tant ses marges peinturez,
Son cuir fleur delizé, & ses bords sur-dorez :
Que rien il ne nous chant d' apprendre la lecture
De ce texte disert." (Edn. Rouen 1602, p. 32.)

The parallel is noticeable in this connection in Sonnet xi. ll. 5-8 (Astrophel and Stella).

So much for the original and after-editions of the Poems. We have to notice next,

II. *The texts of our edition, punctuation aud line-arrangement, classification, &c.*

The posthumousness of all the editions of Sidney's Writings, as explained, together with the semi-furtive character of the first 'printing' of nearly all, compels an Editor to sit in judgment on the entire available texts; and this is no slight task, as the 'various readings' are very abundant throughout.

To begin with 'Astrophel and Stella,' as incomparably presenting Sidney at his best as a Poet, independent of its priceless biographic interest and heart-revelation, this set of Poems, we have seen, was first published in 1591 in such a form as led Mr. Collier to pronounce it 'surreptitious'—as already noted. We cannot go this length; for, as will appear immediately, with all its errors, it must have been printed from authoritative though early transcript MSS. Our collations show that the alleged 'innumerable errors' of Nash's quarto (1591) were in the greater number of instances not errors, but variant readings from earlier MSS. than the second quarto (in part); and also show that the second quarto, which has been so exalted over the first, is, to a large extent, simply a reprint of the first. It is also found that the 'Arcadia,' &c. vol.

of 1598 (not of 1593, as usually stated) fulfils the promise of 'H.S.', that the Countess of Pembroke would publish Sidney's Defence of Poetrie and his Poems. In the second quarto of 1591 nothing was added to the first quarto. This was for the first time done in the 'Arcadia,' &c. of 1598, viz. Sonnet xxxvii., part of Song viii., part of x., and all Song xi. Neither were any of the scattered pieces added until 1598.

Notwithstanding all this, the Nash quarto of 1591 was certainly disapproved by some who claimed to interfere. The proof of this is found in the Stationers' Register, under the date of 18th September 1591, where we read: 'Item, paid to John Wolf, when he ryd with an answere to my L. Treasurer, beinge with her majestie on progresse, for the takinge in of bookes intituled Sir P. S. Astrophel and Stella.'[2] It is scarcely possible to pronounce as to the particular edition here indicated. For (*a*) it is to be remarked that the first, or so-called 'surreptitious' edition (of 1591) spells 'Syr,' not 'Sir,' as in the Register entry; while the second edition (of 1591) spells, as in the entry, 'Sir.' (*b*) It seems not unlikely that Newman sought to hinder Matthew Lownes—who afterwards published

[2] Mr. Collier, as before.

Sidney complete, *e.g.* 1613 (folio)—from issuing his edition, which, as we have stated, is in the Britwell copy also dated 1591, though without date in the Bodleian copy. (*c*) It does not harmonise with an absolutely 'surreptitious' publication, that the Publisher of it was also the Publisher of the alleged authorised edition (Thomas Newman). Further, when we come to examine the first edition of 1591, along with the second edition, it is discovered that the second has errors not found in the first, as well as the first errors which are corrected in the second. But above all, I must reiterate a previous fact, viz. that the alleged authorised second edition to a large extent was dependent on the first, and continues and aggravates its mispunctuation, &c. Our Notes and Illustrations place this beyond dispute. The objection was probably twofold. (1) A number of the added Sonnets in the first edition were by Samuel Daniel, a friend of the Countess of Pembroke, as of Sidney. He may therefore for personal reasons have urged on the family the fact that Sir Philip Sidney's fame might suffer from the Nash edition being printed from a transcript of the Sonnets in their earlier and less revised form. There is an element of doubt here, in that Daniel may have himself contributed the added

Sonnets, and so aided in the Nash edition. (2) The Countess of Pembroke may have shrunk, on the one hand, from the over-laudation of her by Nash; and on the other, we can understand that the association of the Earl of Oxford (Sidney's insulter), along with 'other diuers noblemen and gentlemen,' with her brother's Poems would be anything but agreeable to her.

Our text of 'Astrophel and Stella' is that of Arcadia edition 1598; but with a constant critical comparison with the 1591 separate editions and the 'Arcadia' texts onward. Wherever we depart from 1598 text (as above), reasons are given in relative Notes and Illustrations; and repeatedly it will there be seen that the first edition furnishes admirable readings, and also that of 1613.

Our text of the 'Certaine Sonnets,' entitled by us 'Sidera,' and of all the Poems from the 'Arcadia' itself—the latter never before collected—is fundamentally that of 1613; with like continuous collation of the texts of 1598 onward, as shown in the Notes and Illustrations. We attach much weight to the folio of 1613, as it is the only edition known to have been in the library of the Countess of Pembroke. Among Heber's books (from Mason's and the Duke of Grafton's collections) was a copy of this 1613 edition, in old morocco, and with the initials of the Countess of Montgomery, and the following inscription: 'This was the Countesse of Pembroke's owne book, given me by the Countesse of Montgomery her daughter, 1625. Ancram.' This has been erroneously described (by Mr. Hazlitt, *s. n.*) as 'the dedication-copy.' The edition has no special dedication, simply the original one by Sidney himself. It was *the* edition selected for her own library by the sister of Sidney; and I have traced other gift-copies of the same edition. From 1598 (folio) there was little or no change beyond orthography; but 1613 appears to us to give, as a whole, the best text of the whole Writings of Sidney. Nevertheless we have not hesitated to accept occasional readings from 1598 and others—all as stated in the Notes and Illustrations in the places.[3]

---

[3] The 1593 Arcadia does not contain the Poems. As stated elsewhere in these remarks, H. S. in 1593 refers to the intention of the Countess of Pembroke to do what was done in 1598 Arcadia, viz. reprint the 'Defense' and the 'Poems.' Hence 1598 text was throughout authorised by the Countess; and all after it (including our adopted text of 1613) adhered closely to its readings—inevitable errors excepted. Examination of the 1598 text shows that its Poems were printed from a revised copy of Q 2, the main changes being in the orthography, line-arrangement, and punctuation.

Our sources for the minor Writings are specified in their several places, and do not call for further notice here. The punctuation of all the editions is arbitrary and uncritical, over and over confusing the construction and perverting the sense. We have spent no little pains on it, and we hope not without success.[4] Let any who may differ from us spend even half an hour in examining any text, early or modern, with ours, and we do not fear the verdict. Our Notes and Illustrations fur-

---

[4] The punctuation, as stated above, is constantly bad, and sometimes wholly wrong. The Arcadia of 1598 made numerous alterations in the punctuation of Q 2, but often erroneously, and in 2 qu. and it, (;) and (:) are thrown in anyhow and anywhere. One thing that seems to have led to a wrong punctuation in A. (1598) and all the Arcadia editions, was the division of each Sonnet into sets of 4 and 4, 3 and 3 lines, divided by spaces, and the consequent tendency of the punctuator to make each division end with a strong stop. It is impossible to punctuate Sidney's sentences with the (.) and (,) of modern punctuation, but the excessive use of (;) and (:) can be much reduced, and I have done it. In one part only is a stronger than ordinary punctuation necessary. The Sonnets end somewhat after the manner of the Epigrams,—that is, with a clause which is either intentionally different from the rest, or a summing-up,—and was often meant to come in the manner of a surprise, or with a previous pause. Hence (:) or (,—) are frequently required.

nish reasons for many of our constructions and punctuations. In the arrangement of the lines in 'Astrophel and Stella,' and the Sonnets generally, we have returned to the solid printing, *i.e.* making the beginning of all the lines range. The 1591 line-arrangement in all the three editions, and even in 1613, is mechanical; viz. (in 1613):

that is, two quatrains and two of three lines, with the 1st, 5th, 9th, and 12th projecting, although the rhymes are 1st and 3d, 5th and 7th; 2d and 4th, 6th and 8th; 9th and 11th, and 10th and 12th, and 13th and 14th. This is the usual structure; and it will be observed that the line-arrangement pays no heed to it, nor to the thought as it flows on. Passionate as are these remarkable Sonnets, they are finished with subtlest art and a reminiscence of Petrarch;[5] and those separated from 'Astrophel and Stella' (in our 'Sidera'), as 'Certaine Sonnets,' owe their separation apparently to their non-Petrarchian form, and departure from the form of the rest of the series. Be this as it may, it is as English Sonnets we study them, and it had been mere pedantry to have adhered to the artificial line-arrangement of the original or other early editions. Nor less so, I opine, to have wasted pains in separately arranging each according to the rhyme-words or endings. I am glad to be supported in this by Charles Lamb in the 'Last Essays of Elia,' in his delicious paper on 'Some Sonnets of Sir Philip Sidney';[6] and in our own day by the present Archbishop of Dublin (Trench) in his 'Household Book of English Poetry' (1868), in his quotations from

---

[5] Sidney's usual arrangement of the tercets are (1) 9 rhymed to 11, 10 to 12, 13 to 14: (2) 9 rhymed to 10, 11 to 13, 12 to 14: neither of which arrangements is found in Petrarch; nor does he authorize the arrangement 9=13, 10=11, 12=14 (Sonnet xxix); so that strictly the only Sonnet in Astrophel and Stella on the Petrarchian model is Sonnet xciv. But in the deeper elements of passion and graciousness, Sidney constantly recalls Petrarch.

[6] More of this paper onward. It is in all the editions of Lamb: ours is 4 vols. 12mo, 1855, vol. iii. pp. 332-341.

Sidney.[7] Similarly I have placed the Eleven Songs of 'Astrophel and Stella' at the close by themselves, as in 1591 editions. Granted that Petrarch introduces among his Sonnets the like, as also Lord Brooke in 'Cœlica,' and Earl of Stirling in 'Aurora,' none the less does such introduction interrupt the flow of the thought and snap the links of the marvellous story.[8]

---

[7] See pp. 27, 28.

[8] It does not appear that the departure from the original arrangement of placing the Songs at the close proceeded on any certain principle. Looking at their distribution, (1) There is no apparent connection between Song i. and any Sonnet preceding or following it. It is placed after Sonnet lxiii. The same may be said of Song iii., which is placed after Sonnet lxxxiii. (2) The second Song (after Sonnet lxxii.) is clearly on the same subject, and, in all probability, of the same date with a marked point in the history of Sidney's love, the kiss spoken of in the succeeding Sonnets lxxiii. lxxiv. lxxix. lxxx. lxxxi. and lxxxii. So that Song iv. fits-in after Sonnets lxxxiv. and lxxxv., which are supposed to have been written on the journey. Song v. appears to agree with, and to coincide in date with its preceding Sonnet, lxxxvi. The 6th Song does not, and with Song vii. may be placed with Songs i. and iii. This last, viz. vii., refers to a meeting not spoken of in the Sonnets, and different from that narrated in Song iv.; for that was at night; this, as shown by st. i. 14 and 15, to one in the daytime. The 9th Song connects itself with viii., and with its succeeding Sonnet (lxxxvii.) on which see relative note. The 10th agrees with this time and Sonnet xcii., and Song xi. agrees with that absent presence (see relative note),

In the other Poems I have adhered substantially to the line-arrangement and otherwise of 1613 (as before). Exceptions are noted in the relative places. Subsidiary points bearing on our text come up in the Notes and Illustrations.

It only remains that in this division of our Essay I give a detailed account of a supposed autograph MS. in the British Museum (15,232), which, as containing a number of the Sonnets of 'Astrophel and Stella,' together with other Verse, demands critical examination, all the more that we have been constrained to pronounce it comparatively valueless.

The MS.—which I shall immediately describe from the sale-catalogue—appears to be in its original green

---

which, as I think, begins as far back as Sonnet xciii., and is certainly continued in Sonnets cv. cvi. I have an idea that both in the Sonnets and Songs there was an intentional irregular intermixture, with a view to present them as poems simply, not as the record of an actual and intense love-story. Stella was still living, it must be remembered, and saw various editions of 'Astrophel and Stella' and the Sidera Poems. The latter carry the same passion with them as do the Astrophel and Stella Sonnets. The '*Ring out, wild Bells,*' which Tennyson has caught up in his 'In Memoriam,' and related pieces (xvii. to xix.) invite commentary. They are all autobiographic in the most pathetic and truthful way.

paste-board cover, and the paper and water-mark (of which anon) are the same in all.

At bottom of *verso* of cover, written when the book was upside down, is '6 Janry. . 32'—the 3 plain, the 2 more doubtful. This seems a different handwriting from any in the MS. Before it, in another hand, is an illegible word.

There are at least six handwritings in the body of the MS.:

(*a*) Scraps of Latin, which, by appearance and subject, I judge to be the hand of a youth learning philosophy.

(*b*) 'A most careless content' (p. 9 *v.*); 'The truth' (p. 10); 'Love by the beams' p. 12 *v.*)—all apparently one hand,—the last somewhat doubtful.

(*c*) A heavier, well-formed, regular, and angular hand.

(*d*) A similar hand, yet clearly different. The ink faded to red-brown.

(*e*) 'Iffe that,' &c. (p. 19)—of which onward.

(*f*) The Astrophel and Stella Sonnets.

(*g*) On one of the blank leaves between the earlier and later Sonnets is what I take to be written as a young person's 'copy' or trial of penmanship.

In making out this list I have been confirmed in my

own conclusions by experts at the British Museum, and by the repeated examination of the MS. by Dr. Brinsley Nicholson.

Passing from ourselves, the MS. is thus described in the sale-catalogue of Benjamin Heywood Bright, Esq. (June 18th, 1844):

'240. Sidney (Sir Philip), Astrophel and Stella, Sonnets, 4to; *injured by damp.*

'*⁎* The following is Mr. Bright's note in this manuscript:

"I suspect that this MS. volume belonged to Wilton —that there is in it the writing of Sir P. S. and his sister. The Sonnets are with corrections made after the first edition, 1591, which is very incorrect. This MS., if I am right, is quite inestimable.—B. H. B."

'Inserted is an autograph letter of Mary Sidney, Countess of Pembroke, intended to show the similarity of portions of the manuscript, which is in various hands, to her writing. Mr. Bright supposes that a part of it is the autograph of Sam. Daniel. The volume contains sixteen of the Sonnets, and some of the Songs of Astrophel and Stella, with other poems not there printed.'

In our priced copy of the Catalogue there is placed against this MS. 4*l.* 14*s.* 6*d.* (Sir F. Madden), a price in such contrast with Mr. Bright's 'inestimable' as to indicate that experts stood in doubt of the manuscript. Nor can it be wondered at; for a collation speedily reveals errors in the 'Astrophel and Stella' Sonnets that could only belong to a transcript, and that a very careless one : *e.g.* in Sonnet i. l. 2, 'thee' (deer thee) for 'the dear She' (2 quartos); 'she' (dear She), A (see our note *in loco*); Sonnet i. l. 8, 'showers' (2 qu. and A) begun as 'flowers'; Sonnet ii. l. 3, 'mind' ('tract,' Q 1) for 'mine' (Q 2 and A); Sonnet iv. l. 4, 'with that it' ('that' impossible); Sonnet iv. l. 10, 'in thee' for 'in me' (2 qu. and A); Sonnet vii. l. 13, 'even' for 'ever' (2 qu. and A); Sonnet viii. l. 2, 'First' for 'Forst' (2 qu. and A); Sonnet x. l. 5, 'in sight' for 'unused' (Q 1); 'inside' (Q 2 and A); Sonnet xv. l. 7, 'dcessed' for 'decessed '=deceased; Sonnet xviii. l. 12, 'doth'—first two letters begun wrongly—query as 'to' and then altered; ibid 'bent' and altered to 'bend'; Sonnet xix. l. 3, 'witts' for 'fruits' (2 qu. and A; see our note *in loco*); Sonnet cv. l. 1, 'light' for 'sight' (2 qu. and A; and see our note *in loco*); ibid l. 12 'did *drive so fast* resist'— the italics erased, being taken in error from next line; Sonnet cvi. l. 13, 'bald' (erased)—bad; Sonnet cvii.

(above *drive so fast*: your strife)

l. 7, on—where an error was about to be committed and the pen drawn down.

These may suffice. With reference to Sonnet i. l. 2, it will be observed that if the first 'thee' stand for 'the' (a spelling found nowhere else in the MS.), then the ( ) is ridiculous, this being only required with the variant reading 'she' (dear she, A). This first 'thee' is perfectly distinct in the MS.; but the paper having been stained and injured, there remains only -hee of the second, th- being just in the position of the thick cross-stroke of the *t*. It does not correspond with the transcriber's 's,' and had an 's' been there, some more of it would have remained. This error and that of Sonnet ii. l. 3, 'mind' for 'mine,' settles to us the non-authority of the 'Astrophel and Stella' portion of the MS. Its transcriber copied, in all probability, from a scribbled and confused prior transcript. A glance shows that it is not in Sidney's autograph, neither in the Countess of Pembroke's; and the same holds of the songs introduced into 'Astrophel and Stella.' The 'variations,' called by Mr. Bright 'corrections,' of 1591 are either errors or inferior and conjectural. The only exception is in Song viii. st. ii. l. 1, 'Astrophil' for 'Astrophel,' which is certainly more accurate as = lover of Stella; but 'Astrophel,' as it was Spenser's, so was it Sidney's spelling, no doubt to disguise the 'love.' These Songs in the MS. are unintelligently left unpunctuated.

Mr. Bright suggests that Daniel's handwriting is in the MS.; but a comparison of the MS. in the British Museum to which he refers (lxxii. not xxii.) satisfies us that this is a mistake. The handwritings are quite distinct. The undoubted autograph-letter of the Countess of Pembroke inserted has nothing resembling it in the MS.; nor in all the six handwritings of the MS. am I certain of any being Sidney's own, with the (somewhat doubtful) exception of a poem (at least verse) on folio 19 as onward. The water-mark looks here and throughout like

W

P S

If the W be not simply a part of the shield, it might be = Wilton, and P S = Philip Sidney. But would Sir Philip Sidney have paper specially marked thus for himself? The handwriting of the now to be noticed Verse has a certain resemblance to Sidney's more careless hand, as in his Letters at Hatfield and elsewhere, examined by myself. But it seems almost impossible that he could be the author (or copyer) of

such Verse. We have done our utmost to decipher
the MS., and it follows literally :

Iffe that [stained] [p]ynes and dyes
Bye dasling of your Eys,
    humblye entreatethe
To staye your selfe, soe lounge
Till you haue harde his songe,
    Whom Cupid beatethe.
Licke to the sillye swanne,
When Line noe more she Cane,   sing
    Settes fourthe her voyce,
Soe I a simple swanne,   swaine
thoughe mortall be my name,
    seeme to rejoice.
When you haue hard his dittie
Whose faythe maye drawe your pitt e
    because vnfayned,
Judge then Whatte he dothe saye
and beare his name a waye
    [illegible] as disdained.
Your eies, licke starres, hathe wroughte
dirrections on my thoughte,
    Thoughte true to you.
O [stained and illegible] the desiers
W^h to my [illegible] aspiers
    tend all to you,
The cares wch nighte dothe bringe
beginne and end one thinge.
    Would Silvya knowe,

Woulde Silvya knowe his faythe
that sundrie sorrowes hathe,
  Or Silvyas Loue.
Woulde Silvya harde his mone,
Who comeforte findeth none
  But Silvyas gloue.
But when he moste dothe murne,
then moste she seames to scorne,
  destinie dismale.
I followe, but she flies,
Neuertheless to please her eyes,
  thancke fortune for all.
Blame not her mynde divyne
Whoe sees wth Wisdome eyen
  howe to make choise.
Thye selfe a waveringe yoothe,
She thinkes thoughte all not trueth,
  that woemens wise.
Whome your beautie and his owne
fortune hath madde forlorne
Bye wch I for [stained]
my woorke of everaie daye
  Wourke to you done.
Your Lookes more fyner seene,
Then of the silkworme ben,
  Careles and comelie.
folde me soe faste all waie
I cannotte breake awaie
  Simple and homelye.
your voice still devidinge,
pearles and rubies shininge,

a wondrous glorie.
[illegible] sweeter smelles by farre
    then flowers ever bare
        in field or storie.
To wch voyce line [?] heuenlye ever
    moste humblye shall p'sever
        in all obedience.
Mye selfe my flocke I keepe,
    Whether I wake or sleepe,
        Wth out resistance.

Turning back to st. ii. l. 5, can the line, 'thoughe mortall be my name,' carry in it a play on the name of Sidney's friend *Dye*-r ? The poem is unworthy even of him ; most certainly has no sign of Sidney in it.[9]

If this Poem be in Sidney's own handwriting, then it is all of his handwriting that is in the MS. ; and if it be not, then most assuredly there is not a single line or word of his handwriting in the whole MS. In our Notes and Illustrations in the places, we make occa-

---

[9] With reference to the occurence and re-currence of 'Silvaya' in these lines, my friend J. M. Thomson, Esq., Edinburgh, asks: "Could this be by the poet whom Sir John Davies (Vol. i. p. 212, Grosart's edn.) calls 'Salue's sad louer true'? The metre there seems to require a trisyllable in place of Salue, and Siluia or Silvaya is near enough."

sional references to the readings of this MS.; but we cannot regard it as at all authoritative. Further details were supererogatory.

So far as I have been able to ascertain, there does not appear to be known a single MS. of the Poems of Sidney in his own autograph, with the small exception of the Lines with Queen Elizabeth's lock of hair, preserved at Wilton. Letters abound in many collections (British Museum, Penshurst, Hatfield), but no MS. of his Poetry.

I proceed to consider

III. *The story of Lady Rich and Sidney in the morale of it, with hitherto unprinted Letters.*

To the Biographer rather than to an Editor belong most of the facts and problems (not to say paradoxes) of the love-story of Sidney and the dazzling 'Stella.' But interpenetrated as are the Sonnets of Astrophel and Stella and the Sidera set of Poems, with the passion of their love and disappointment, joy and most tragic sorrow, it seems an inevitable task even to an Editor to touch on certain points, seeing that our great and good memories are too few to be lightly left to traditionary mistake and misconstruction, if these be removeable.

Fundamentally it must never be forgotten that the chronology of these Love-Sonnets and Poems is at present perplexing; that is to say, they have from the first been put together without regard to their *nexus*, very much apparently as the scattered originals or transcripts came into the hands of their first publisher, Thomas Newman—for his order (or dis-order) was scarcely departed from afterwards. They thus came to be printed merely as so many Sonnets and Poems, as an addition to the Poetry of England—then meagre—with no reference to the two hearts that were laid bare in them. It is of the last importance to remember this; for upon the dates of these Sonnets and Poems is contingent our verdict of shame or praise; and shame has been too readily pronounced. *E. g.* there are Sonnets that, though placed onward, seem to belong to a very early period, while ' Stella ' in heart and hand was still free and to be wooed. Others similarly placed, that is misplaced, onward, self-revealingly belong to the inter-space during which only the sacred memory of her father's dying prayer for their union held them; when Sidney was not 'enthralled' by her, nor she by him. Others, placed hither and thither, belong to a time when Sidney's

MEMORIAL-INTRODUCTION.

heart was filled to its utmost capacity with his love for Stella, though Leicester's marriage made him fear she was being removed by circumstances beyond his winning. Then there are others that were born of the unexplained fact that she had married another, unworthy of her; and coördinate with these, others that belong to the discovery of a '*forced*' marriage, of a hand-loss without a heart-loss, and all the consequent anguish and tumult. Finally, there is a double set, also misarranged hither and thither, belonging to (*a*) the struggle with a love known to be in her heart and his own inextinguishable and burning love; (*b*) the recovery and victory of both, after a keen, intense discipline. So too with the 'Sidera' set: they seem to have been intentionally intermixed and sundered.

Some day surely something of the thought and love given to Shakespeare's Sonnets will be dedicated to those of Sidney; and if so, the story hidden in them be relieved of stains and shadows at present resting on it.[1]

---

[1] Sonnets xxiv. xxxv. and xxxvii. are much too early placed in the series: xxv., again, is too late. So too v. xxx. xl. and xli. are self-evidently misplaced. A very noticeable Letter to Languet, in the 'Zurich Letters' of the Parker Society, shows that in March 1578 Sidney was not yet 'enthralled' by his love for Stella. I

Throughout, a study of these Sonnets and Poems impresses us not merely with the brilliant beauty and splendid intellectual gifts of 'Stella,' but profoundly with her self-restraint and her restraint of Sidney. The rebuke of her adorer for a stolen kiss (Sonnet lxxiii.) is only one of very many semi-unconscious admissions

must find room for a short extract, premising that the Editor (Dr. Robinson) supplies Lady Penelope Devereux's name in the place as the 'illa': 'But I wonder, my very dear Hubert, what has come into your mind, that when I have not as yet done anything worthy of me, you would have me bound in the chains of matrimony; and yet without pointing out any individual lady, but rather seeming to extol the state itself, which, however, you have not as yet sanctioned by your own example. Respecting her, of whom I readily acknowledge how unworthy I am, I have written you my reasons long since; briefly indeed, but yet as well as I was able. At this present time, indeed, I believe you have entertained some other notion; which I earnestly entreat you to acquaint me with, whatever it may be: for everything that comes from you has great weight with me; and to speak candidly, I am in some measure doubting whether some one, more suspicious than wise, has not whispered to you something unfavourable concerning me, which, though you did not give entire credit to it, you nevertheless prudently, and as a friend, thought right to suggest for my consideration. Should this have been the case, I entreat you to state the matter to me in plain terms, that I may be able to acquit myself before you, of whose good opinion I am most desirous; and should it only prove to have been a joke, or a piece of friendly advice, I pray you nevertheless to let me know

on Sidney's part that Stella, while owning her kindred 'love' for him, stood true and inviolate. This does not appear to have been sufficiently weighed in behalf of Essex's radiant sister. Neither has the fact of that kindred love been sufficiently weighed on behalf of Sidney. It must have been a terrible discovery on each side. Terrible to Stella, that she was the enforced wife of Rich, while her 'love' was still Sidney's; terrible to Sidney, that he had that 'love,' while she was Rich's. Leicester's marriage had cut off his presumptive inheritance of *his* wealth and position, and apparently Sidney had concluded that the love was only on his side, and that, infinitely deeper than he ever suspected until it was 'too late'; and when he did discover that the love was co-equal in her, and that nevertheless she could not now be his, very awful must have been the conflict between honour and love, heart and conscience. There was an enormous amount of justification of the struggle, of the slow-

immediately, since everything from you will always be no less acceptable to me than the things that I love most dear.' (Zurich Letters, 2d series, p. 297; Latin, p. 182: dated 1st March, 1578.) Sidney seems to suspect that even thus early he was being talked of in relation to Stella—to suspect, indeed, that it was regarded as a moral necessity that he should marry some one.

ness utterly to yield each other up. I cannot apportion the praise of the ultimate triumph as between Stella and Sidney. I find in Sonnets lxxxvii. lxii. and elsewhere, demonstration that the triumph was not all on one side, and that side Sidney's. One line is laden with pathos : 'Alas, I found that she with me did smart !' I have an abiding conviction that while Sidney lived, 'Stella' was true and pure and noble, after no common ideal, and in every way worthy of Sidney. I give to Stella without reserve the glory of having 'kept' Sidney true to his best self. She opened his eyes to discern the wrong path he was taking in still seeking to cherish a hopeless love for her. She drew from him that great cry of pain—to me unutterably piercing—'*nowe of the basest.*' [2] It was a love-tragedy

[2] See our relative note. I am satisfied that Sonnet xiv. belongs to the same period, and is much too early placed in the series. Lines 4-8 are profoundly suggestive of a consciousness of wrong-feeling, not the less so that there is a semitone of defiance in the answer:

'ye must contend
To grieue me worse, in saying that Desire
Doth plunge my wel-form'd soule euen in the mire
Of sinfull thoughts, which do in ruin end.'

Like internecine heart-struggles are revealed all through the later Sonnets. I note the following as worthy of study: v. ll. 1-4, 13-14; x. ll. 7-11 ; xvi. l. 10; xviii. ll. 8-12 ; xix. ll. 3-6 ; xx.

more lamentable than ever even Shakespeare or Philip Massinger (Sidney's 'Philip') imagined; and over the after-years of Stella, for myself I have infinite pity and nothing but tears. I fear the 'fine bells' were 'jangled' under the terrible sorrow of her brother's death. For Sidney, I dare not say with Shelley in 'Adonais,'

> 'Sidney, as he fought
> And as he fell, and as he lived and loved,
> Sublimely mild, a spirit without spot';

echo of Spenser's earlier,

> 'Nor Spite itself, that all good things doth spill,
> Found aught in him that she could say was ill.'
> (Astrophel.)

He was human, and therefore there were 'spot' and 'ill'; but it is as though one caught the music of the spheres amid the dissonance of a thunderstorm and comet-haunted air to find Sidney, released of his unwarranted and impossible 'love,' thus singing at last:

> 'Leave me, O Love, which reaches but to dust,
> And thou, my mind, aspire to higher things;

l. 14; xxi. l. 4 and 7; xxv. l. 14; xxviii. l. 8; xxxiv. l. 2 and 14; xxxvii. l. 11; xlvii. l. 12-14; l. lii. lxi. lxii. lxvi. lxix. lxx. lxxii. lxxiv. lxxxiv. lxxxvii. xc. xci. xcii. xciii. civ. and cix.

Grow rich in that which never taketh rust;
Whatever fades, but fading pleasure brings.
Draw in thy beams, and humble all thy might
To that sweet yoke where lasting freedoms be;
Which breaks the clouds, and opens forth the light,
That doth both shine, and give us eyes to see.
O, take fast hold; let that light be thy guide
In this small course which birth draws out to death;
And think how ill becometh him to slide,
Who seeketh heav'n, and comes of heavenly breath.
Then farewell, world; thy uttermost I see :
Eternal Love, maintain thy life in me !'
                                    (A. and S. cx.)

Looking a little closer to the Sonnets of 'Astrophel and Stella,' certain dates are recoverable. Bourne (p. 286) fixes Stella's marriage in 1580 ; but, as Lloyd has very well shown (pp. ix. x.), the Letter of Lord Huntingdon, on which he relies in departing from 1581, corrects his error. It is indorsed '10th March, 1580,' which by our calendar is 1581. Consequently Stella could not have been married till after the 10th March 1581—it may have been well on in 1581. 'The error,' observes Lloyd (p. x.), 'is the more grave that Mr. Bourne's estimate of Sidney's moral character depends upon it.' By the true date we have an enlarged period for the Love-Sonnets as having been composed while 'wooing' was still innocent.³

Turning to Sonnet xxxiii., it is usually supposed that Sidney here speaks of Stella's marriage, and laments his error in not marrying her. I ask the student-reader to open at this Sonnet and read it slowly. This interpretation seems altogether opposed to facts and to the wording of the Sonnet itself. There was no 'might be.' Leicester's marriage had rendered Sidney unacceptable to her friends, and it is nonsensical to suppose a 'might be' when they so 'forced' her marriage that she proclaimed her dislike at the very altar, and—in vain. This too being the case, how, if Sidney meant to refer to the marriage, could he have written of himself:

> 'No force, no fraud rob'd thee of thy delight,
> Nor Fortune of thy fortune author is'?

Besides, while there is only very conjectural evidence

---

³ Lloyd's proof is incomplete, because 10th March 1580 by Lord Huntingdon might have been our 10th March 1580. The official indorsement X March 1580 decides it, because officials kept to the official commencement of the year. The copy of Constable's letter in Cotton MSS. is in point. Constable dates 9th Jan. 1604, and we learn that he dated as we would, by the official indorsement 1603.

that Sidney was so smitten with her before the marriage, or that he himself knew the power she held over him until the shock of the marriage came, there is the evidence of the larger proportion of the Sonnets to show that it was not till late in the period comprised in the Sonnets that he was aware she loved him. The tone of the Sonnet, the word 'day' in l. 4, explained as it is by its repetition in ll. 12-14, the 'respects' spoken of in l. 11, and most of all ll. 12-14, show that he is merely lamenting that slanderers should talk that he showed so much respect to her and to himself as to absent himself on some especial occasion when he might have met her. 'Fitly-punisht eyes' agrees with this, but is an absurd phrase if he were lamenting his loss in not marrying her; and the whole of this early Sonnet—except in so far as 'In respects' shows an early phase of her love—is similar to, and may be profitably compared with, Sonnet cv. on a somewhat similar occasion. Very trivial things in love were then magnified.

In Sonnet xxiii. l. 1, the 'some' and 'others' and and l. 7 show this to have been composed after his return to Court in or about October 1580. How long after is another question.

Sonnet xli. is a very noticeable one chronologically.

On Whit-Monday 15th May 1581, after hasty but great preparations, a gorgeous tournament was held by and before Queen Elizabeth, in honour of the French Ambassadors who had arrived to treat of her marriage with the Duke of Anjou. Sidney was one of the challengers who attacked the fortress in which Queen Elizabeth, as the Queen and Virgin Beauty, was enthroned. The Sonnet may not, it is just possible, refer to this time and event; and unfortunately, though a long account of it was printed, neither the Author, nor Holinshed, who copied from it, mention the prize-winners. But, looking to the greatness of the occasion, it is most probable that the Sonnet does refer to it; for had Sidney been vanquished, then he would hardly boast of those French and English having been spectators and awarders of the minor prize of some ordinary tilting, the very mention of which has not come down to us.

Sonnet xxx. is dated by Pears and others in the Spring of 1580, thus placing it several months earlier than Sonnet xxxiii., even on the supposition that the latter was written on Stella's marriage. But Languet's letters to Sidney are decisive as to a later date. Writing on the 28th October 1580, he says: 'The Archduke Mathias has heard from Vienna that peace is made between the Turks and Persians, and letters from Constantinople imply the same, but do not directly affirm it. They add that the Sultan has commanded Ochiali to have a number of new galleys built, so that it is expected he will make some attempt against the Spaniards next Summer. It certainly concerns him in the highest degree that the Spaniards should not conquer Portugal, lest they should deprive Egypt of their traffic with India through the Red Sea,' &c. Now Languet's intelligence was likely to be as early, if not earlier than any that got abroad at Cork; nor is it probable that the report as to the Turks would have got abroad earlier than the cessation of the year's campaign at the time of going into winter-quarters. So long as the Persian war lasted, the Sultan could not have undertaken a European one, and, as it turned out, the Persian war did go on; and therefore the intention, if intention there were, of going to war with Spain came to nothing. Hence the date of the Sonnet necessarily falls between the middle, say, of Nov. 1580 and June 1581, and the words 'this year' rather point to some early month in 1581. With regard to the Polish War, Languet's news of 21st November 1579 shows that Stephen could not then have been meditating invasion, as he had only just recovered Polotzk, and was beseiging Smolensk. Similarly, on 6th February 1580 he writes (Pleskow being then beseiged by Stephen): 'The Muscovite prince is said to be at Pleskow (*i. e.* for its relief) with a large force, with which it is expected he will invade Livonia.' Late in the year, I think on 24th September, he mentions a report that Stephen had been killed by his own people; and in October, immediately after the quotation about the Turks, adds: 'What we heard about the death of the King of Poland is not true. They say he has penetrated with his victorious army into the heart of Muscovy, and that the Muscovite is suing to him for peace.' The query therefore that Sidney alludes to was probably whether Stephen would again enter Muscovy or make peace. 'Muscovy' seems to have had a strange interest for Sidney. It is introduced into the earliest of the Sonnets. Had he a prophetic glimpse of the after-offer of Poland's crown to him?

These remarks may go to show the need of a very thorough revision of the chronology of 'Astrophel and Stella' and related Poems.

It is now my privilege to print for the first time no fewer than five letters from Stella as Lady Rich and as Countess of Devonshire. I found these at Hatfield while pursuing other researches there by the unreserved permission of the Marquis of Salisbury. Such letters, if intrinsically not very remarkable, cannot but be of interest to all who care to get nearer to great historic names; and certainly 'Stella' has 'for all time' taken her place in the heaven of Literature beside not merely the Geraldine of Surrey earlier, or the Mary of Robert Burns later, but with the Laura of Petrarch, and Beatrice of Dante, and Rosalind and Elizabeth of Spenser, and Celia of Carew, and Castara of Habington, and Leonora of Milton, and Sacharissa of Waller.

These Letters, and a very touching and noble one to Elizabeth in behalf of her brother (Essex), published by us in 'The Farmer Chetham MS.,' for the Chetham Society, are exceedingly characteristic in their gracious light-heartedness and kindly interest in the humblest.

The first is addressed to the Earl of Southampton —Shakespeare's Southampton[4]—as follows:

---

[4] I have for some years been collecting materials for an adequate Life of Shakespeare's Southampton. These prove more abundant than has been supposed. Ere very long I expect to put them into shape.

'Noble S^r, I hope my first letter will excuse some parte of my faulte, and I assure you nothinge shall make me neglecte to yealde you all the ernest assurances I can of my affection and desires to be helde deare in your fauour, whose worthy kindnes I will striue to merit by the faithfullest endeuors my loue can performe towards you, who shall euer finde me vnresumably,

'Your Lo. faithfull cosin and true frende,
'PENELOPE RICH.

'Your Lo. Daughter is exceeding faire and well, and I hope by your sonn to winn my wager.

'Chartly, this 10 of May.'

It is indorsed 'The La. Rich: to ye E. of Southampton;' and has a note, 'This alludes to the expectation the Earl had of a son at this time. See Lodge.' The seal is a 'deer,' very much resembling that used by Andrew Marvell later.

Our next Letter is also addressed to Southampton:

'The exseeding kindnes I resue [receive] from your Lo. in hering often from you doth geue me infinite contentment, bothe in refering assurance of your health and that I remaine in your constant fauor, which I well enduour to merit by my affection unto your Lo. my Lo. Riche doth so importune me dayly to retorne to my owne house as I can not stay here longar then bartelmentide, which I do against his will, and the cause of his ernest desire to haue me come vp is his being so persecuted for his lande, as he is in feare to loose the greatest parte he hath and his next terme, who would haue me a soliseter to beare parte of his trobles, and is much discontented with my staing so longe : wherefore I beseche your Lo. to speeke with my brother, since I am lothe to leue my La. here alone, and if you resolue shee shall go with me into Essex, which I very much desire, then you were best to write to me that you would haue her go with me, which will make my Lo. Riche the more willing, though I know he will be well contented, to whom I haue writen that I will come as soone as I knowe what my Brother and your selfe determins for my Lo. I am sorry for Sir Hary Bauers hurte, though I hope it is so littel as it will not marr his good face; and so in hast I wishe your Lo. all the honor and hapines you desire.

'Your Lo. most affectionat cosin,
'PENELOPE RICHE.

'Chartly, this 9 of iuly.
'To the most honorable the Earle of Southamton.'

'Chartley,' it will be remembered, was the first meeting place between Stella and Sidney.

Our third Letter is far onward, being indorsed 'La. Rich, 1604.' It follows :

'Mr. Renalls, my ould woman harny hath a sute to my brother, which I would not haue her troble him with; but that it is only his letter to my Lo. Maire [Mayor] for a meane place that is fallen in his gifte, which she desires for her sonn White. Let me intreate you to drawe a letter, and that some body may go if you haue no laisor

[leisure] your selfe, that will be ernest with the Maire, since it is like he will excuse it if he can for some creature of his owne; and so in haste I rest,
 'Your very assured frende,   PENELOPE RICHE.
'To my frende Mr. Renalles.'

Our next is to the Earl of Salisbury, and thus runs:

'Noble Lo., this Jentell woman hath intreted me to recomende her sute vnto you, of whose good sucses I should be very glade, because she is on [one] I haue bine longe aquainted with, and is of the best disposition that euer I founde any of her nation. I beseche your Lo. to fauour her, that if it be possible she may obtaine some satisfaction if her desires be not vnreasonable; and so wishing your Lo. all happines and contentment, I remaine,
 'Your Lo. most affectionate frende to do you seriuce,
             'PENELOPE RICHE.
'Ennile[?], this last of May. [Indorsed ' 1605.']'
'To the right honorable my Lo. the Earle of Salisburye.'

Our last Letter is of peculiar interest, as being from Stella as the Countess of Devonshire. It is as follows, and is also addressed to Salisbury:

'Noble Lo., the rumers of your sicknes I confes hath made me hast to this place, wher I might resue [receive] better satisfaction by the knowledge of your health, and had the good fortune this day to meet with the messenger you sente to my Lo. of Clanricarde, whereby I was assured of your safe recouery, beseeching your Lo. to beleue that no frende you haue liuing doth participate more of your grefe or ioye then my selfe, whose affection you haue so infinitly obliged with your constante fauours. while I was at draiton with my mother, the yonge hunters came very well pleased, vntill your seruant came with your comission to gide my Lo. of Cranborne to my La. of Darbye, which discont'ment for feare of parting three days made them all loose their suppers, and became extreeme maliciouse, till it was concluded that ther traine should staye at Draiton, and they go to gether with to [two] seruants a peece. I feare nothing but ther riding so desperately, but your sonn is a perfett horse man, and can nether be out riden nor matched any waye. my mother, I thinke, will growe yonge with ther companye : so longinge to here of your safe and perfect health, I remaine

'Your Lo. most faithfull to do you seruice,
P. DEUONSHIERE.
'Wansted, this Monday.'

It is indorsed 'Lady Deuonshire, 1606,' and addressed 'To the right honorable my Lo. the Earle of Salisburye.'[5] These Letters and the whole story of

[5] By the kindness of the Marquis of Westminster I was favoured with a contemporary transcript (1616) of Mountjoy's, *i.e.* Devonshire's, defence of his marriage with Lady Rich. It proved to be a mere technical and scholastic defence of marriage of a divorced wife during the lifetime of her former husband. There is not a scintillation of personal reference. Numbers of copies are extant.

Stella, earlier and later, strongly tempt to commentary and 'Apology'—in its old sense. I cannot too emphatically re-utter my own conviction, after anxious study of it under no common advantages, that Stella in her relations with Sidney was, if anything, the truer and nobler. Spenser saw nothing but glory in the passionate story:

> 'To her he vow'd the service of his days;
>   On her he spent the riches of his wit;
>   For her he made hymns of immortal praise;
>   Of only her he sung, he thought, he writ;
>   Her, and but her, of love he worthy deem'd;
>   For all the rest but little he esteem'd.'
>   (Astrophel, ll. 61-66.)

It seems to me about the shallowest of criticism imaginable that says, as does the Archbishop of Dublin in his Notes to his charming 'Household Book of English Poetry' (as before) : 'Sir Philip Sidney's sonnets may be "vain and amatorious," as Milton has called his fine romance of The Arcadia, but they possess grace, fancy, and a passion which makes itself felt even under the artificial forms of a Platonic philosophy'; and then emptying out the meaning of the right word 'passion,' goes on : 'They are addressed to one who, if the course of true love had run smooth, should have been his wife. When, however, through the misunderstanding of parents, or through some other cause, she had become the wife of another, Platonic as they are, they would far better have remained unwritten' (pp. 390-1). Nay, verily! Our early Literature is not so rich as to afford the loss of 'Astrophel and Stella' and related Poems, while 'Platonic' is about the most inept and false description of the 'passion' one could conceive. It was, I believe, a tragedy of Conflict, and the Love went down to the very roots of both in their deepest. Earlier there was pastime and intellectual exercise, or, as Sonnet i. (Astrophel and Stella) puts it, 'studying inuentions fine her wits to entertain'; but as you read you find yourself borne on a molten stream of love-passion. I know nothing grander than the double overcoming of it. To call such a struggle of Love and Honour, Heart and Conscience 'Platonic' shows—with the profoundest respect for his Grace—in our estimate, a revelation of sad ignorance or momentary forgetfulness of the facts and the persons. To the last, Sidney was 'bound' to Stella; for I fear she who became his wife was utterly unworthy of him, whether regarded intellectually or womanly. Perhaps Mrs. Craik in her passionate 'Head of the Family' has best put the feeling that I imagine to have remained with Sidney, as follows : 'Let no one say that passion is unconquerable. It can never be so in a pure heart. Inevitable necessity—the stern sense of right—the will at last bent to that holier Will which maps out human life—can in time crush-down the individual longing that would wholly appropriate to itself what seems fairest both to its spiritual and visual eye. Yet nothing can obliterate tenderness—that hallowed lingering of memory which seems to say, "Thou art not mine,—I have ceased to hope or even wish it so; but no one can ever be to me in thy stead, and at any time I would give my life to pour out blessings upon thee and thine." With this sort of feeling, strangely intense though calm, Ninian went to see Mrs. Ulverston' (c. xxxiii.). I pass finally to

IV. *The characteristics of Sidney's Poetry, with the praises of it by his contemporaries and onward.*

We have already called attention to the *posthumous* publication of the entire Writings of Sidney. To this falls now to be added the undoubted fact that 'Astrophel and Stella' and the 'Sidera' and kindred Poems never were intended for the public—were for 'Stella' alone, save in the earlier and lighter, wherein Sidney played with her love after the manner of his age. No one ought to come to the study of his Poetry without an abiding recollection of this. There are things in every man's life which are not for the world's eyes. There are things especially that lose their subtlest edge of meaning—as a handled peach or plum its bloom—when read as mere written words. There are things too that grow unconsecrate if their inner message be made outer.

Regarded broadly, the Poetry of Sir Philip Sidney has three characteristics that I wish briefly to set forth : (*a*) Passion ; (*b*) Thought ; (*c*) Fineness of art.

(*a*) *Passion.* This requires only a very few additional sentences to what has been already submitted. The man just as he was is self-painted as in a diary in 'Astrophel and Stella'; and throughout, Sidney was intense in all he did. His letters—as the memorable one to ' Mr. Molyneux ' and the imperishable one to Queen Elizabeth—in especial show this ; but most of all, his Poetry. You miss the sweetest music of 'Astrophel and Stella,' if you do not steep your own spirit in the passion of its Sonnets and Songs. And so is it everywhere. You have the throbbing heart, the quick conscience in its tremor and disturbance and seeking of the right, the shifting moods, the sudden freaks of fancy, the overbearing grief, the as overbearing ardour, the frank penitence, the as frank avowal of failure to master, and, sounding out like a muffled buoy-bell, cries of absolute distress that are to me awful. The Poetry of Sidney is marked by this Passion because into his Poetry he has put the most of his own very self, at his best and worst, noblest and basest—for there was the 'base' too. Occasionally the Passion hides itself in strangely artificial forms—just as a splendour of tree-blossom and tree-fragrance was often and often found while the trees were clipped and over-trimmed in very fantastique of gardening art; but taken all in all, there is Passion in this Poetry, that informs it as the blood does our body; and hence a life, a mobility, an electric excitation of sympathy, almost unique.

(*b*) *Thought.* This Sidney shared with his friend Fulke Greville, Lord Brooke, and indeed all his foremost contemporaries. The reserve of power in these Poems is something wonderful. You feel that what is uttered is as nothing to what is left unuttered. You are held by a sense of Thought 'too deep' for words. If Passion, *i.e.* Feeling, as distinguished from Thought be the predominant characteristic, certainly Thought in quantity and quality is a second characteristic that the most cursory reader of these Poems cannot fail to be struck with. You have it in most unlooked-for places. As a whole—but only as a whole—the Poems of 'Arcadia' are not up to the high intellectual level of 'Astrophel and Stella' and 'Sidera' set. Yet as you 'search' and ponder them you are astonished at ' the superficiality and haste of that criticism which has. read so poorly the 'thoughts that breathe and words that burn' of these 'Arcadia' poems. There is, apart from their brilliance imaginatively and vivid nature-portraiture, some of Sidney's deepest and most unique thinking in them. Take this blending of affection and aspiration in his celebration of Stephen Languet:

'The song I sang old Languet had me taught,
Languet, the shepherd best swift Ister knew;
For clarkly read, and hating what is naught,
For faithful heart, clean hands, and mouth as true,
With his sweet skill my sailless youth he drew
To have a feeling taste of Him *that sits
Beyond the heaven, far more beyond our wits.*'

Or take this glimpse of his sounding of the 'depths of things' in a snatch burdened with thick-coming questionings:

'What essence destiny hath! if fortune be or no;
Whence our immortal souls to mortal earth do stow;
What life it is, and how that all these lives do gather
With outward maker's force, or like an inward father.
Such thoughts, methought, I thought, and shamed my
      single mind,
Then void of nearer cares, the depths of things to find.'

I have cited these in preference to others marked and re-marked by the score, that I might adduce Dr. George Macdonald's comment on them (in 'Antiphon,' p. 79), as follows: 'Lord Bacon was not the only one, in such an age, to think upon the mighty relations of physics and metaphysics, or, as Sidney would say, "of naturall and supernaturall philosophie." For a man to do his best, he must be upheld, even in his speculations, by those around him. In the specimen just given, we find that our religious poetry has gone down into the deeps. There are indications of such a tendency in the older times, but neither then were the questions so articulate, nor were the questioners so troubled for an answer. The alternative expressed in the middle couplet seems to me the most imperative of all questions, both for the individual and for the Church. Is man fashioned by the hand of God, as a potter fashioneth his vessel; or do we indeed come from His heart? Is power or love the making might of the universe? He who answers this question aright possesses the key to all righteous [query—religious?] questions.'

The Poetry of Sir Philip Sidney is packed with Thought of this deep, interrogative-speculative type; nor does he fail to suggest the true answers. The poorer and most artificial of the 'Arcadia' poems come first. We felt constrained to adhere to the original order of the pieces; but it is a disadvantage. Let the reader simply read and pass on from No. i. to vi. and other after-poems of considerable extent. Those onward will yield unexpected treasure of aphoristic thoughts, epigrammatic sayings, proverb-like condensations of trains of observation, felicitous compliments, dainty-coloured epithets, arresting metaphors, and many celebrations of old English manners and customs pricelessly valuable. I cull from literally hundreds of marked passages these, which are all in a single poem:

A RURAL BEAUTY.

'Neuer the Earth on her round shoulders bare
A maid train'd up from high or low degree,
That in her doings better could compare   equal
Mirth with respect, few words with curtesie,
A carelesse comlinesse with comelie care,
Selfe-gard with mildnesse, sport with majestie.'
                         (x. Lamon, ll. 209-14.)

PURSUED LION.

'Strephon so chas'd did seeme in milke to swimme;
He ran, but ran with his eye ore shoulder cast,
More marking her than how himselfe did goe:
Like Numid lyons by the hunter chas'd,
Though they doe flie, yet backwardly do glowe
With proud aspect, disdaining greater haste.'
(Ibid ll. 288-93.)

LOVE-SMITTEN.

'A shot unheard gave me a wound unseene.'
(Ibid l. 455.)
'Mine eyes had their curse from blessèd eyne.'
(Ibid l. 497.)

Cf. this, 'Who where she went beare in her forehead Morning' (xxx. Strephon, &c. l. 70). Again, and deeper:

GOD.

'To harme vs wormes should that high Iustice leaue
His nature? nay, Himselfe? for so it is:
What glory from our losse can He receaue?
But still our dazled eyes their way do misse;
While that we do at His sweete scourge repine,—
The kindly way to beate vs on to blisse.'
(xviii. Plangus, &c. ll. 67-70.)

These must suffice. Finally here—Nowhere have you the high*est* genius without some sense of humour. I should have liked to have dwelt on this additional characteristic of Sidney's thought. I must content myself by referring to the 'Mopsa' (i. and lxxviii.) pieces. These will satisfy that, with all his loftiness and gravity, Sir Philip could and did discern the 'wit' in men and things—exactly as a close study of even Milton and Dante, George Herbert and Cowper, show that they had this faculty of humour, and could laugh at as well as with the 'humours' of their fellows.

(c) *Fineness of art.* I have no intention to intermeddle with the 'Areopagus,' as Spenser called it, wherein Gabriel Harvey, Sir Edward Dyer, Fulke Greville Lord Brooke, Sidney, and Spenser, sought to found a new school of poetry. We are not as yet sufficiently furnished with information on either the design or the methods contemplated. The merest fragments of detail have reached us. The actual specimens of 'classical rhythms,' as distinguished from the 'encumbrance of rhyme,' are puzzles on all sides. Nor are the hexameters of the 'Arcadia' the least incomprehensible. Certes it had been a poor exchange to have given the 'Faerie Queen' for Spenser's iambics, or 'Astrophel and Stella' for Sidney's hexameters and other vagaries. Thomas Nash, who had wealth of admiration for Sidney and Spenser, if contemptuous hate for Harvey, adjudged well, when he pronounced in the well-known quotation, that though the hexameter verse 'be a gentleman of an ancient home, yet this clime of ours he cannot thrive in. Our speech is too craggy for him to set his plough in. He goes twitching and hopping in our language, like a man running upon quagmires, up the hill in one syllable and down the dale in another; retaining no part of that stately smooth gait which he vaunts himself with amongst the Greeks and Latins.' Even Spenser himself could poke fun at the experiment, ultimately; *e. g.* it is 'either like a lame gosling that draweth one leg after, or like a lame dog that holdeth one leg up.'

Passing these 'experiments'—which neither Southey nor Longfellow have been able to revive—our Notes and Illustrations of 'Astrophel and Stella' and the 'Psalmes' demonstrate in the amount of various readings with what insistence of care and with what daintiness and fastidiousness of election Sidney matured his Verse. If the reader will keep a look-out for it, he will again and again be arrested by the exquisite art and delicacy of many of these Poems. Even his most rapturous as his most troubled Sonnets of 'Astrophel and Stella' have cunning workmanship. It were idle to point out examples. I wish to suggest study, and to guide to insight.

Considering that when the well-nigh innumerable Elegies were issued upon his death scarcely a line of his Poems had been printed, it is noticeable that, with hardly an exception, he is celebrated preëminently as a POET. 'He was the Muses' joy'; give him 'the laurell, *with the bay*;' 'crowned with lasting bays'; and

> 'Did never Muse inspire beneath
> A Poet's brain with finer store';

and the like, perpetually occur. Then Spenser in his plaintive Pastoral thus sang:

> 'He could pipe, and dance, and carol sweet,
> Amongst the shepherds on their shearing feast;
> As summer's lark, that with her song doth greet
> The dawning day, forthcoming from the East.
> And lays of love he also could compose:
> Thrice happy she whom he to praise did choose.'

And his sister, in her inestimable 'Doleful Lay of Clorinda,' calling on the shepherd-lasses to wear 'cypress' instead of flower-garland, asks 'Who ever made such lays of love as he?' Ben Jonson has celebrated similarly,

'That taller tree, which of a nut was set
  At his great birth, *where all the Muses met*';

and Thomson caught up the flying echo :

'Nor can the Muse the gallant Sidney pass.
  The plume of war ! with early laurels crowned,
  The lover's myrtle, and *the Poet's bay*.'

It were easy to multiply recognition of Sidney as a Poet by the foremost of our Literature—to trace Shakespeare's reading of him with wondrous assimilative sympathies, and so others ; and yet our Fuller Worthies' Library edition was the first collective and adequate edition of his Poetry. This, while among the 'British Poets' and 'Lives of the Poets' the merest rhymesters have found an apparently irremovable place.

I should measure a man's capacity by his estimate of Sidney as man and poet, and equally of the poet as of the man. No one who has sympathy with our supremest Singers can neglect him. Very nobly has Mr. Ruskin written of him in his *Fors Clavigera* (Letter xxxv.), as thus :—" If you don't like these love-songs, you either have never been in love, or you don't know good writing from bad, (and likely enough both the negatives, I am sorry to say, in modern England)."

I cannot find room unfortunately for the eloquent sequel—somewhat mistaken in its data, but most powerful—on the circumstances in which 'Astrophel and Stella,' and other love-verse were rooted and nurtured. The student-reader will gladly turn to the complete Letter. But this is the close :—" Thus died, for England, and a point of personal honour, in the thirty-second year of his age, Sir Philip Sidney, whose name perhaps you have heard before, as well as that of his aunt-in-law, Lady Jane Grey, for whose capital punishment, as well as that of the Duke of Northumberland, (his grandfather,) her mother, as above stated, was in mourning when he was born. And Spenser broke off his Faery Queen for grief when he died; and all England went into mourning for him ; which meant, at that time, that England was really sorry, and not that an order had been received from Court." [6]

[6] It may be noted here that Mr. Ruskin quotes and praises characteristically " Highway, since you my chief Parnassus be " and " I see the house ; my heart, thyself contain ! " and " All my sense thy sweetness gained." Of the first, on " Hundreds of years you Stella's feet may kiss " he exclaims : " Hundreds of years ! You think that a mistake ? No, it is the very rapture of love. A lover like this does not believe his mistress can grow old, or die." Of the third he says: " And here is one more, written after a

I cannot more fitly close our Essay than with Charles Lamb on 'Some Sonnets of Sir Philip Sydney.' It is excursive in the outset, and I excise a digression on Milton; but here is all the rest, as follows:

'Sydney's Sonnets—I speak of the best of them—are among the very best of their sort. They fall below the plain moral dignity, the sanctity, and high yet quarrel, which is the prettiest of all as a song; and interesting for you to compare with the Baron of Bradwardine's song at Lucky M'Leary's." In an earlier letter (xxiii.) Mr. Ruskin penetratively discerns Sidney's full genius in his " Psalmes," as elsewhere, *e. g.* " Please note that your next number of *Fors Clavigera* ought to be in the hands of your readers on Friday, the 1st, or Saturday, the 2nd of November. The following day being Sunday, the 3rd, there will be read in every church in England, or in the world, where the Church Service is used, the 15th Psalm, which distinctly declares the man who shall ascend to God's holy hill to be him who, amongst other things, has not put forth his money upon usury; a verse impiously ignored in most of the metrical versions of the Psalms; those adapted to popular tunes or popular prejudices. I think, accordingly, that some of my readers may be glad to have a sounder version of that Psalm, and as the 14th is much connected with it, and will be variously useful to us afterwards, here they both are, done into verse by an English squire,—or his sister, for they alike could rhyme; and the last finished singing what the brother left unsung, the Third Fors having early put seal on his lips." [This doubt as to the authorship is put at rest by us earlier.] "You may not like this old English modest spirit of self-approval of Milton, in his compositions of a similar structure. They are, in truth, what Milton, censuring the Arcadia, says of that work (to which they are a sort of after-tune or application), " vain and amatorious" enough, yet the things in their kind (as he confesses to be true of the romance) may be "full of worth and wit." They savour of the courtier, it must be allowed, and not of the Commonwealthman. But Milton was a courtier when he wrote the Masque at Ludlow Castle, and still more a courtier when he composed the Arcades. When the national struggle was to begin, he becomingly cast these vanities behind him ; and if the order of time had thrown Sir Philip upon the crisis which preceded the Revolution, there is no reason why he should not have acted the same part in that emergency which has glorified the name of a later Sydney. He did not want for plainness or boldness of spirit. His letter on the French match

at first; but if you can find anybody to read it to you who has an ear, its cadence is massy and grand, more than that of most verse I know, and never a word is lost. Whether you like it or not, the sense of it is true, and the way to the sacred mount, (of which mounts, whether of Pity, or of Roses, are but shadows,) told you for once, straight-forwardly,—on which road I wish you Godspeed."

VOL. I.   f

may testify he could speak his mind freely to princes. The times did not call him to the scaffold. The Sonnets which we oftenest call to mind of Milton were the compositions of his maturest years. These of Sydney, which I am about to produce, were written in the very heyday of his blood. They are stuck full of amorous fancies, far-fetched conceits, befitting his occupation; for true love thinks no labour to send out thought upon the vast and more than Indian voyages, to bring home rich pearls, outlandish wealth, gums, jewels, spicery, to sacrifice in self-depreciating similitudes, as shadows of true amiabilities in the beloved. We must be lovers—or at least the cooling touch of time, the *circum præcordia frigus* must not have so damped our faculties as to take away our recollection that we were once so—before we can duly appreciate the glorious vanities and graceful hyperboles of the passion. The images which lie before our feet (though by some accounted the only natural) are least natural for the high Sydnean love to express its fancies. They may serve for the loves of Tibullus, or the dear Author of the Schoolmistress [Shenstone], for passions that weep and whine in Elegies and Pastoral Ballads. I am sure Milton never loved at this rate.' [The word 'Sydnean' reminds us to intercalate that Richard Crashaw in his marvellous 'Wishes to his supposed Mistresse' dedicates one vivid stanza in it to our Sidney :

'Sydnæan showers
Of sweet discourse, whose powers
Can crown old Winter's head with flowers.']

After quoting and criticising one of Milton's addresses (in Latin), 'Ad Leonaram,' Elia proceeds : 'I am sure Sydney has no flights like this. His extravaganzas do not strike at the sky, though he takes leave to adopt the pale Dian into a fellowship with his mortal passion.' He then gives Sonnet xxxi., remarking, ' The last line of this poem is a little obscured by transposition. He means, Do they call ungratefulness there a virtue ?' The further sonnets quoted are xxxix. xxiii. xxvii. xli. liii. lxiv. lxxiii. lxxiv. lxxv. ciii. and lxxxiv. And the reader will do well to follow Elia's guidance, and give an hour to the studying of these sonnets. He continues : ' Of the foregoing, the first [xxxix.], the second [xxiii.], and the last [lxxxiv.] sonnet, are my favourites. But the general beauty of them all is, that they are so perfectly characteristical. The spirit of "learning and of chivalry"—of which union Spenser has entitled Sydney to have been the "president"— shines through them. I confess I can see nothing of the "jejune" or "frigid" in them; much less of the "stiff" and "cumbrous"—which I have sometimes heard objected to the Arcadia. The verse runs off swiftly and gallantly. It might have been tuned to the trumpet, or tempered (as himself expresses it) to "trampling horses' feet." They abound in felicitous phrases:

"O heav'nly Fool, the most kiss-worthy face."

"Sweet pillows, sweetest bed;
A chamber deaf of noise, and blind of light;
A rosy garland, and a weary head."

"that sweet enemy,—France."

But they are not rich in words only, in vague and unlocalised feelings—the failing too much of some poetry of the present day; they are full, material, and circumstantiated. Time and place appropriates every one of them. It is not a fever or passion wasting itself upon a thin diet of dainty words, but a transcendent passion pervading and illuminating actions, pursuits, studies, feats of arms, the opinions of contemporaries, and his judgment of them. An historical thread runs through them, which almost affixes a date to them; marks the *when* and *where* they were written.' It needeth not now that we add Lamb's reply to Hazlitt's paradox of insult.

And so it is a joy to me to invite all genuine students of our early literature to give days and nights to the noble Verse of Sir Philip Sidney, now collected for them. Mary, Countess of Pembroke, as she wept over that 'immortal spirit,' sobbed:

> 'Ah, me, can so divine a thing be dead?'

and answered, of faith:

> 'Ah, no! it is not dead, nor can it die,
> But lives for aye in blissful paradise.'

Nor in a 'blissful paradise' only. For long as England lasts will Sir Philip Sidney's name be her boast and ornament. My work for the present has been mainly on his Poetry, and I close with Matthew Roydon's prescient as loving estimate of the Man and the Poet:

> 'You knew—who knew not Astrophel?
> (That I should live to say I knew,
> And have not in possession still!)—
> Things known permit me to renew—
>   Of him you know his merit such,
>   I cannot say—you hear—too much.

Within these woods of Arcady
He chief delight and pleasure took;
And on the mountain Partheny,
Upon the crystal liquid brook,
　The Muses met him every day,
　That taught him sing, to write, and say.

When he descended down the mount,
His personage seemed most divine:
A thousand graces one might count
Upon his lovely cheerful eyne.
　To hear him speak, and sweetly smile,
　You were in Paradise the while.

A sweet attractive kind of grace;
A full assurance given by looks;
Continual comfort in a face;
The lineaments of Gospel books—
　I trow that count'nance cannot lye,
　Whose thoughts are legible in the eye.

　　*　　*　　*　　*　　*　　*

Alas, all others this is he,
Which erst approvèd in her song,
That love and honour might agree,
And that pure love will do no wrong.
　Sweet saints, it is no sin or blame
　To love a man of virtuous name.

Did never love so sweetly breathe
In any mortal breast before;

*Did never Muse inspire beneath
A Poet's brain with finer store.*
He wrote of Love with high conceit,
And Beauty rear'd above her height.'
                                ALEXANDER B. GROSART.

∗∗* I add here two of Henry Constable's Sonnets on Lady Rich, prefacing that Ben Jonson thus praised him :

'Hath our great Sidney Stella set
Where never star shone brighter yet?
Or Constable's ambrosiac muse
Made Diana not his notes refuse?'

I. TO THE LADIE RICH.

'Heralds at armes doe three perfections quote,
  To wit—most faire, most rich, most glittering ;
  So when these three concurre within one thing,
Needs must that thing of honour be, of note.
Lately did I behold a rich faire coate,
  Which wishèd fortune to mine eyes did bring :
  A lordly coate—but worthy of a king :
Wherein all these perfections one might note—
A field of lilies, roses proper bare,
  To stars in chiefe, the crest was waves of gold ;
How glittering was the coate the starrs declare,
  The lilies made it faire for to behold ;
And rich it was, as by the gold appears,
So happy he which on his armes it beares.'
                                (Diana : Son. x.)

II. TO MY LADYE RICH.

'O that my songe like to a ship might be,
   To beare aboute the world my Ladie's fame;
That, chargèd with the riches of her name,
The Indians might our countrye's treasure see.
No treasure, they would say, is rich but she;
   Of all theyre golden parts they would have shame,
   And haplye, that they might but see the same,
To give theyre gold for nought they would agree.
This wishèd voyage, though it I begin,
   Without your beautie's helpe cannot prevayle:
For as a ship doth beare the men therein,
   And yet the men doe make the ship to sayle,
Youre beauties so, which in my verse apeare,
Doe make my verse and it your beauties beare.'

(Sonnets from Todd's MS. p. 6: Hazlitt's edition of Constable, 1859, pp. 7, 39-40.) There are other two Sonnets on Lady Rich by Constable: (*a*) 'A calculation upon the birth of an honourable Ladie's daughter, borne in the yeere 1588, and on a Friday' (p. 18); (*b*) 'Of the death of my Ladie Riche's daughter: shewing the reason of her untimelye death hindred her effecting those things which by the former calculation of her nativitye he foretold' (p. 44).

I.
ASTROPHEL AND STELLA.

NOTE.

The Student-Reader will find in our Essay in the present volume, full details on the following points:

(*a*) The original and after-editions, and the Bright MS. (of a portion) of Astrophel and Stella.

(*b*) The text of our edition, line-arrangement and rhyme-structure, punctuation, &c.

(*c*) The chronology and arrangement of the Sonnets, and the admixture of the eleven Songs (so-called) with them—removed to end in our edition.

(*d*) The story of Lady Rich and Sidney—with hitherto unprinted Letters—in the *morale* of it.

In their places Notes and Illustrations of the cx. Sonnets and xi. Songs are given. In these Notes and Illustrations, Q 1 is = Nash's edition of Astrophel and Stella (1591 40): Q 2 = the second edition, without Nash's Epistle (1591 40): 2 qu. = the two editions of 1591 : A = Arcadia, edition of 1598, and A 1613 = the Arcadia, edition of that year. On these and other editions see Essay, as before. At the end of these there are a few longer Notes (*a* to *h*) which would have overcrowded the pages; and as Notes *i*, and *j, e, k*. 1. the Epistle-dedicatory of the Publisher of the first edition of Astrophel and Stella, 1591 ; 2. the Epistle-prefatory of Thomas Nash in the same; 3. the Preface to Arcadia, &c. of 1593.

Throughout I have supplied headings for the successive Sonnets, drawn from the leading thought of each, and in the Poet's own words. It is found that the absence of headings is inexpedient in the case of most readers. I have also printed these and the after-Sonnets in solid, not after the erratic arrangement of lines in the early Arcadia editions and others. But see a critical account of the line-arrangement, &c., as *supra*. G.

ASTROPHEL AND STELLA.

I.

' Looke in thy heart, and write.'

LOUING in truth, and faine in verse my loue[1] to show,
That she, deare Shee,[2] might take som pleasure of my paine,—
Pleasure might cause her reade, reading might make her know,
Knowledge might pitie winne, and pitie grace obtaine,—
I sought fit wordes to paint the blackest face of woe ;
Studying inuentions fine, her wits[3] to entertaine,
Oft turning others' leaues, to see if thence would flow

---

[1] 2 qu. read 'my love in verse.'
[2] In 2 qu. 'the dere Shee': earlier and less passionate: Bright MS., 'thee (deer thee).'
[3] Preferable to 'witte' Q 2, as including imagination, fancy, &c.

Some fresh and fruitfull showers[4] vpon my sun-burn'd
   brain.
But words came halting forth,[5] wanting Inuention's
   stay;   support
Inuention, Nature's childe, fledde step-dame Studie's
   blowes;
And others' feete still seem'de but strangers in my way.
Thus, great with childe to speak, and helplesse in my
   throwes,   throes
Biting my trewand[6] pen, beating myselfe for spite; truant
Foole, said my Muse to me, looke in thy heart, and write.

II.

' Love gave the wound.'

NOT at the first sight, nor with a dribbed[1] shot,
   Loue gaue the wound, which, while I breathe,
      will bleede;

---

[4] It was more than one 'shower' that he looked for, and the plural agrees with 'words' and 'inventions,' ll. 5, 6; better therefore, than 'shower' of 2 qu.

[5] 2 qu. 'out.' Changes noted above indicate that this and l. 1 are later variants by the Author.

[6] "You are no *trewant* in the Law, I see"; Lod. Barrey's "Barn Alley" (1636), act i. sc. 1.

[1] = a term in archery, which has been ill explained (Measure for

But knowne worth did in mine[2] of time proceed,
Till, by degrees, it had full conquest got.
I saw, and liked; I liked, but loučd not;
I loued, but straight did not what Loue decreed :

Measure, act i. sc. 4). As it appears to be the primitive of the frequentative 'dribble,' and allied to drip, drop, and droop, I agree with Mr. Collier's explanation, and take the sense here to be—not with a weak shot elevated that it may reach the mark during its fall, but with a straight-driven aim. Steevens' quotation from Ascham (Toxoph. p. 94, Arber's reprint) may be thus explanatorily filled in: Ascham (Tox.) says that be a man never so apt to shoot, or never so well taught in his youth, 'yet if he giue it ouer, and not vse to shote,' [then when through pleasure or war he betakes himself to it again] 'he shall become, of a fayre archer, a stark squyrter and dribber.' 'Dribbed' = 'dribb'd,' is more expressive of weakness than 'dribbèd' (A), and the tense agrees better with 'gave' than Q 2.

Reverting to l. 1, we read:

'Not at | first sight | nor with | a drib | bing (Q 2) / bed (MS.) shot' |

'Not at | the first | sight nor | with a | dribbed (=dribb'd) shot.' (A)

'Not at | the first | sight nor | yet with | a dribbed shot.' (A, after editions.)

Of these I prefer A, because the second clause is lighter to sound, and so more in agreement with the sense. The third reading seems to be one where 'yet' was inserted, but 'the' or 'a' inadvertently retained.

[2] In Q 1 'tract.' 'Mine' might perhaps be = 'mean' *i.e.* through

At length, to Loue's decrees I, forc'd, agreed,
Yet with repining at so partiall lot.
Now, euen that footstep of lost libertie
Is gone; and now, like slaue-borne Muscouite,[3]
I call it praise to suffer tyrannie;
And nowe imploy the remnant of my wit
To make myselfe beleeue that all is well,
While, with a feeling skill, I paint my hell.

III.
' All my deed but copying is.'

LET dainty wits crie on the Sisters nine,
    That, brauely maskt, their fancies may be told;
Or, Pindare's apes, flaunt they in[4] phrases fine,

---

the instrumentality of time; but from the word 'conquest,' the reference seems to be to the slow, unsuspected, yet very sure, advance by mining, then as now much used in sieges. See Alexander of Parma's Campaigns in the Low Countries, &c. Hence it seems later than 'tract' of Q 1. The Bright MS. has 'mind': cf. ix. 13.

[3] It is the glory of the present Czar to have ended the long-continued serfdom of so many of his subjects.

[4] = let them flaunt, may they. Our modern taste would prefer A and Q 2, 'flaunt in their': but the choice must be decided by l. 4.

ASTROPHEL AND STELLA. 9

Enam'ling with pied flowers their thoughts of gold;[5]
Or else let them in statlier[6] glorie shine,
Ennobling new-found tropes with problemes old;
Or with strange similes enrich[7] each line,
Of herbes or beasts which Inde or Affrike hold.[8]
For me, in sooth, no Muse but one I know;
Phrases and problemes from my reach do grow;

[5] Q 2, '*their pride with flowers of gold*,' seems at first sight the better; but there is the objection that in the enamelled jewels of that day—the then style from which this metaphor is taken—it was not the enamel that was enamelled with gold, but the gold that was enamelled with coloured paste. Hence Q 2 and A reading is a later alteration, though not a happy one, the less so that 'Pindare's apes' was not altered. This phrase we must take not in a depreciatory but good sense, just as 'imp' was then used in a sense very different from its present meaning. Cf. 'O sleep, thou ape of death' (Cymbeline, act ii. sc. 2), where there is no intended depreciation of sleep, but rather admiration of the resemblance to the calm placidity into which the troubled features mould themselves. In this line '*pied*' is = parti-coloured.

[6] *i.e.* more stately than mine, not more stately than the style of Pindar and his imitators. The 'stateleyee' of Q 2 I take to be an error.

[7] Q 1, 'inricht': probably a blunder of tense, yet cf. 'maskt,' l. 2.

[8] Alluding to the style exemplified in Lyly's Court Comedies and Euphues (1579?).

And strange things cost too deare for my poore sprites:
How then? euen thus,—in Stella's face I reed
What Loue and Beautie be; then all my deed
But copying is, what, in her, Nature writes.

IV.
' Vertue, thou thy selfe shalt be in loue.'

VERTUE, alas, now let me take some rest;
    Thou set'st a bate betweene my will and wit;[9]
If vaine Loue haue my simple soule opprest,
Leaue what thou likest not, deale not thou with it.
Thy scepter vse in some olde Catoe's brest,
Churches or Schooles are for thy seat more fit;
I do confesse—pardon a fault confest—
My mouth too tender is for thy hard bit.
But if that needes thou wilt vsurping be
The little reason that is left in me,
And still th' effect of thy perswasions prooue,
I sweare, my heart such one shall shew to thee,
That shrines in flesh so true a deitie,
That, Vertue, thou thy selfe shalt be in loue.

[9] Q 1 has '*love* and wit': Q 2 and A 'will and wit.' As Love is an extern deity acting on him (l. 3), and making his 'will' way-

V.

'True beautie vertue is.'

IT is most true that eyes are form'd[1] to serue
The inward light, and that the heauenly part
Ought to be King, from whose rules who[2] do swerue,

ward and an opponent of his wisdom or wit, 'will' is preferable. Breton made the phrase familiar by his 'Will of Wit.' In this line 'bate' is = debate, contention, strife—probably from Fr. '*l'attre*.' Cf. Song vi. l. 1, and Nares and Halliwell *s.v.* for examples: 2 Henry IV. act ii. sc. 4: Countess of Pembroke's Antonius, &c. I would add that, by taking the technical hawking term ' to bate' as allied to this, and as meaning not merely to flutter but to flutter strivingly, a much finer sense is given to the various passages where it is metaphorically employed.

[1] Q 1, 'bound': Q 2, 'found': A, 'form'd.' 'That eyes are *'found'* to serve the inward light and not the outward show, is contrary to fact, and besides is not his own (or his friend's) argument. 'Bound' is probably the earlier reading, though inferior to 'form'd.' The Bright MS. has 'found.'

[2] This is plural. Cf. 'rebels strive' and 'their' (l. 4); and though 'that,' as a collective, often took a verb singular, the examples of a plural 'who' so followed are very rare, and perhaps never when it precedes its own noun. Here the singular 'doth' of Q 2 necessarily makes a modern reader change the plural noun 'rebels' into a verb singular, to the utter confusion of the sense: and as errors of 'do' and doth occur throughout, and as A and the Bright MS., as well as A 1613, give 'do,' I adopt it. The archaic plural in —eth is not used by Sidney.

Rebels to nature, striue for their owne smart.
It is most true, what we call Cupid's dart
An image is, which for ourselues we carue,
And, fooles, adore in temple of our hart,
Till that good god make church and churchmen starue.
True, that true beautie vertue is indeed,
Whereof this beautie can be but[3] a shade,
Which, elements with mortall mixture breed.
True, that on earth we are but pilgrims made,
And should in soule vp to our countrey moue :
True, and yet[4] true—that I must Stella loue.

VI.

' I do Stella love.'

SOME louers'speake, when they their Muses entertaine,
　　Of hopes begot by feare, of wot not what desires,
Of force of heavnly beames infusing hellish paine,

---

[3] 2 qu. 'but be.'

[4] Q 2, 'most.' 'True,' says Sidney, 'all these arguments are true, yet my reply is—I must love Stella.' All previous to this reply are the discussions of his friend, or of his better sense. Hence I prefer 'yet' to 'most.' Cf. S xiv. and xxi. and Letter of Languet. Griffin echoes this in his ' Fidessa.'

Of liuing deaths, dere wounds, faire storms, and frees-
 ing fires:
Some one his song in Ioue and Ioue's strange tales
 attires,
Bordred with buls and swans, powdred with golden
 raine :
Another, humbler wit, to shepheard's pipe retires,
Yet hiding royall bloud full oft in rurall vaine. vein
To some⁵ a sweetest plaint a sweetest stile affords,
While⁶ teares poure out his inke, and sighes breathe
 out his words,
His paper pale despaire, and pain his pen doth moue.
I can speake what I feele, and feele as much as they,
But thinke that all the map of my state I display
When trembling voyce brings forth, that I do Stella loue.

VII.

'Stella's eyes in colour black.'

WHEN Nature made her chiefe worke, Stella's eyes,
 In colour blacke⁷ why wrapt she beames so bright?

---

⁵ =some one. The construction is, A sweetest style affords to some [one] a sweetest plaint.   ⁶ Q 2, 'whiles.'
⁷ Cf. with this sonnet our Sir John Davies, Vol. ii., pp. 239-40,

Would she, in beamy blacke, like Painter wise,
Frame daintiest lustre, mixt of shades and light?
Or did she else that sober hue deuise,
In obiect best to knitt and strength our sight;
Least, if no vaile these braue gleames did disguise,
They, sunlike, should more dazle then delight?
Or would she her miraculous power show,
That, whereas blacke seemes Beautie's contrary,
She euen in blacke doth make all beauties flow?
Both so, and thus,—she, minding Loue should be
Placed euer[8] there, gaue him this mourning weede
To honor all their deathes who for her bleed.

---

two of his poems first printed by us. But in the Poems of Bp. Henry King (1657, p. 6) the first is ascribed to Mr. Henry Rainolds and the second to King. From the position these occupy in the Davies M.S. they can be taken from him without affecting the presumption in favour of the Davies authorship of the others.

[8] Bright M.S. 'euen.' The latter perhaps under influence of 'euen' two lines above, with which thought, however, this one has nothing to do, as shown by 'Both so, and thus.' 'Euer' is no doubt hyperbolical; but that Love should be placed 'euen' in Stella's eyes would be an insult and no compliment.

VIII.

'*Love . . . in my close heart.*'

LOUE, borne in Greece, of late fled from his natiue place,

Forct,[9] by a tedious proofe, that Turkish hardned hart

Is[1] not fit marke to pierce with his fine-pointed dart;

And, pleas'd with our soft peace, staide here his flying[2] race :

But, finding these north clymes too[3] coldly him embrace,

Not vsde to frozen clips,[4] he straue to finde some part

Where with most ease and warmth he might employ his art ;[5]

At length he perch'd[6] himselfe in Stella's ioyfull face,

---

[9] Bright M.S. miswrites 'First.'

[1] Q 1, 'were'—a remnant of the 'hearts' in the same, and not altered in Q 2, while altering = to 'Is.'

[2] 2 qu. 'fleeting' : 'flying' agrees better with the kind of 'race' noted than 'fleeting.'

[3] This from Q 1 seems preferable to 'do,' Q 2 and A and A 1613.

[4] This, from Q 2 and A and A 1613, agrees better with 'embrace' than 'lippes,' Q 1, and shows a more total coldness. Clip = embrace or hug.

[5] Sometimes misprinted 'dart,' as in Gray's Misc. Works and American reprint.

[6] Q 2 misprints 'preach'd.'

Whose faire skin, beamy eyes, like morning sun on[7]
    snow,
Deciu'd the quaking[8] boy, who thought, from so pure
    light,
Effects of liuely heat must needs in nature grow :
But she, most faire, most cold, made him thence take
    his flight
To my close heart; where, while some firebrands he
    did lay,
He burnt vn'wares his wings, and cannot flie away.

IX.
' Vertue's Court.'

QUEEN Virtue's Court, which some call Stella's face,
    Prepar'd by Nature's choysest[9] furniture,
Hath his front built of alabaster pure ;
Gold[1] is the couering of that stately place.

---

   [7] A 1613 has badly ' or.'   [8] *Ibid* 'waking.'
   [9] Here and elsewhere 'chiefest' is changed in A to 'choicest.' Cf. Sonnet x. 24.
   [1] Stella's, therefore, was the strange beauty of a golden-haired blonde with dark eyes. Henry Constable in 'Diana' (Son. x.), 'To the Ladie Rich' sings thus of her :

The doore, by which sometimes comes² forth her grace,
Red porphir is, which locke of pearle makes sure,
Whose porches rich—which³ name of chekes indure—
Marble, mixt red and white, doe enterlace.
The windowes now, through which this heav'nly guest
Looks ouer the world, and can finde nothing such,
Which dare claime⁴ from those lights the name of best,
Of touch⁵ they are, that without touch doe touch,

"A field of lillies, roses proper bare
To stars in chiefe, the crest was waves of gold:"

and see that other to Mr. Hilliard upon occasion of a picture of my Lady Rich, No. 6, p. 45 (Hazlitt's ed. 1859). It was perhaps this peculiarity of golden hair and fair rosy complexion with dark eyes —a peculiarity which would give particular brilliancy and mark to the eyes—that caused Sidney to name her Stella.

² Q 1 has 'runnes,' a mistake for 'rowes' of Q 2: but I prefer 'comes,' A and A 1613, as expressing better that she 'sent forth' her grace or graciousness.

³ 2 qu. misprint 'with,' a not unfrequent mistake in these poems, and elsewhere.

⁴ = dare claim for themselves the name of 'best,' and so dispossess Stella's eyes of that title.

⁵ There is a quibble here throughout. 'Touch,' though used for any costly marble, is properly, says Nares, the *basanitis* of the Greeks, the hard black stone of the Rosetta inscription, and he refers to Dean Vincent's Commerce of the Anc. ii. 534. Hence its

Which Cupid's selfe, from Beautie's mine ⁶ did draw :
Of touch they are, and poore I am their straw.

X.
Reason and Loue.

REASON, in faith thou art well seru'd, that still
  Wouldst brabbling ⁷ be with Sense and Loue in me ;
I rather wisht ⁸ thee clime the Muses' hill ;

use here, for it will be remembered that Stella's eyes were a lustrous black. But in l. 14 he evidently uses the same word in its other meaning, and indicates that her eyes were like lighted tinder or matchlock match, and he the straw that they inflamed. Halliwell, *s.v.*, gives 'Touch-box, a receptacle for lighted tinder carried by soldiers for matchlocks.' 'Touchwood' is |still in use; and cf. Son. xv. l. 10. Sir John Harington seems to have had these lines in mind when he says (Epigr. iv. 91), ' Of a lady in a Straw Hat:
  ' What architect this work so strangely matcht
    An yvory house, doors, walls,—and windows tutch ;
    A gilded roof with straw all over-thatcht.'
⁶ See note on Sonnet ii. l. 3. Here ' mind ' of A is repeated in A 1613 ; but it is ' mine ' in 2 qu. and in the Bright M.S. ' myne.' Yet as Donne rhymes it as ' mind '=mine with ' unkind,' it would appear that ' mind ' is not merely a slip of the pen, but an old though incorrect form of the word, like ' vild.'
⁷ In Bright MS. ' arguing.' Looking to Sidney's frame of mind when he wrote the sonnet, and his view that reason was intermeddling where not wanted, ' brabbling ' seems preferable.
⁸ 2 qu. ' wish.'

Or reach the fruite of Nature's choysest [9] tree ;
Or seeke heav'n's course or heav'n's inside [1] to see :
Why shouldst thou toyle our thornie soile to till ?
Leaue Sense, and those which Sense's obiects be ;
Deale thou with powers of thoughts, leaue Loue to Will,
But thou wouldst needs fight both with Loue and
    Sence,
With sword of wit giuing wounds of dispraise,
Till downe-right blowes did foyle thy cunning fence ;
For,[2] soone as they strake thee with Stella's rayes,
Reason, thou kneeld'st,[3] and offered'st straight to proue,
By reason good, good reason her to loue.

---

[9] Q 2, 'cheefest.' See note on Sonnet ix. l. 2.

[1] The Bright MS. has 'in sight'—an error. The converse error is made in Sidney's Psalmes of Dauid, xvii. 3, l. 2, where we read (from MS.) 'searching *inside* tride.' See in the place.

[2] 2 qu. 'so.'

[3] 'knewest' in 2 qu.: 'kneeld'st,' A. Both give good sense, and as the person is Reason, it is hard to say which is the better. But 'kneeld'st' is perhaps the more forcible and the more agreeable to the custom of the Tilt-yard, whence the whole metaphor is drawn, and it has the appearance of being an after-change, introducing a new image and thought in a passage where the 'knowing' is sufficiently expressed by 'proving by reason good.' I adopt 'kneeld'st.'

XI.[4]

'Love, thou leav'st the best behinde.'

IN truth, O Loue, with what a boyish kind   nature
   Thou doest proceed in thy most serious wayes,
That when the heav'n to thee his best displayes,
Yet of that best thou leau'st the best behinde!
For, like a childe that some faire booke doth find,
With gilded leaues or colourd velume playes,   vellum
Or, at the most, on some fine picture stayes,
But neuer heeds the fruit of Writer's mind;
So when thou saw'st, in Nature's cabinet,
Stella, thou straight lookt'st babies in her eyes,
In her chekes' pit thou didst thy pitfold set,
And in her breast bo-peepe or crouching lies,
   Playing and shining in each outward part;
   But, fool, seekst not to get into her heart.

XII.

'Cupid.'

CVPID, because thou shin'st in Stella's eyes—
   That from her locks[5] thy day-nets none scapes free—

---

[4] See longer note at close (*a*) on this Sonnet.

[5] For 'locks' 2 qu. has 'lookes': for 'day-nets' of Q 2 we have in A and A 1613 'daunces.' Either 'locks' or 'lookes'

That those lips sweld⁶ so full of thee they be—
That her sweet breath makes oft thy flames to rise—
That in her breast thy pap well sugred lies—
That her grace gracious makes thy wrongs—that she,
What words soere shee speake, perswades for thee—
That her cleere voice lifts thy fame to the skies,—

might be used as =Cupid's 'nets' ('day-nets'). For 'daunces' Q 1 misreads 'dimnesse,' and the Bright MS. 'daynties' (which also has 'locks'). A MS. annotator 1674, in one of our copies of Arcadia, gives 'dancet,' a line in heraldry; it is not wavy, but indented or notched or zig-zag, and therefore scarcely applies. The curious thing is, that the word of one agrees better with the opposite word of the other:

'looks ⨯ day-nets
locks   dances.'

As the hair is not otherwise mentioned, I adopt 'locks.' Notwithstanding all this I shall not quarrel with any one who prefers 'her *looks* thy day-nets' seeing [that it is not incorrect to say caught (or snared) *by a look;* and that 'eyes—looks,' balance 'lips—breath' (ll. 3-4). 'Daunces' (A) may be explained by the phrase of the eyes 'dancing with delight.' 'Day-nets' (Q 2) is given in Halliwell on the authority of Diet. Rust [ique] as a net for catching small birds. Query—a corruption of dare or daze-net, where mirrors were used? These being necessarily 'day-nets,' in opposition to night-snares, the corruption was easy.

⁶ =[are] swelled. Another of the not infrequent instances of participles in -ed requiring some part of the substantive verb to be supplied.

Thou countest Stella thine, like those whose powers
Hauing got vp a breach by fighting well,
Crie 'Victorie, this faire day all is ours!'
O no; her heart is such a cittadell,
So fortified with wit, stor'd with disdaine,
That to win it is all the skill and paine.

XIII.

'*Phœbus.*'

PHŒBUS was iudge betweene Loue, Mars, and Loue,
    Of those three gods, whose armes the fairest were.
Ioue's golden shield did eagle sables beare,
    Whose talons held young Ganimed aboue:
But in vert field Mars bare a golden speare,
    Which through a bleeding heart his point did shoue:
Each had his creast, Mars carried Venus' gloue,
    Ioue on his helmet the thunderbolt did reare.
Cupid then smiles, for on his crest there lies
Stella's faire haire, her face he makes his shield,
Where roses guculs are borne in siluer field.   gules
Phœbus drew wide the curtaines[7] of the skies,

---

[7] Q 1, Q 2, 'curtalne.'

To blaze these⁸ last, and sware devoutly then,   blazon
The first, thus matcht, were scantly⁹ gentlemen.

XIV.

'*Alas, haue I not paine enough!*'

A LAS, haue I not paine enough, my friend,
   Vpon whose breast a fiercer Gripe¹⁰ doth tire
Then did on him who first stale down the fire,
While Loue on me doth all his quiuer spend,—
But with your rubarbe¹ words ye must contend,   rhubarb
To grieue me worse, in saying that Desire
Doth plunge my wel-form'd soule euen in the mire

---

⁸ Q 1 and Q 2 and Bright MS. 'the last'—inferior.

⁹ 2 qu. 'scarcely.' As they bore arms, they were gentlemen. Hence A's 'scantly' is preferable, as showing that they were on the borders, but only just within the borders, of that rank. 'Scarcely' infers they had hardly reached the rank.

¹⁰ = (γρύψ), griffin or vulture, says Nares. He should have said 'griffin or eagle,' both because it is applied to the eagle of Prometheus, and because the vulture neither tires with sharp claws nor feeds on living animals, but on carrion; 'tire' = seize with the beak (Fr. tirer).

¹ He says 'rubarb,' because its various kinds, partly from its real effects, and partly from its colour, were supposed to cleanse the liver, and the liver was the supposed seat of desire and fleshly love.

Of sinfull thoughts, which do in ruin end ?
If that be sinne which doth the manners frame,
Well staid with truth in word and faith of deede,
Ready of wit, and fearing nought but shame ;
If that [2] be sin, which in fixt hearts doth breed
A loathing of all loose vnchastitie,
Then loue is sin, and let me sinfull be.

XV.
'Dictionarie's methode.'

YOU that do search for euery purling spring
    Which from the ribs of old Parnassus flowes,
And euery flower, not sweet perhaps, which growes
Neere thereabouts,[3] into your poesie wring ;
Ye that do dictionarie's methode bring
Into your rimes, running in ratling rowes ;[4]
You that poore Petrarch's long-deceasèd woes

---

    [2] Q 2, 'it.' The text preferable. Cf. ' that ' in l. 9. Mistake of y^t=that and y^t=it, common.

    [3] More substantial, and therefore better when 'near' is prefixed than 'thereabout.' 2 qu. and Bright MS.

    [4] Alliteration of 'Dictionaries' or Alphabetical method': and l. 6 sarcastically illustrates this. Dryden has a similar conjunction of rhyming and rattling, though he is not attacking Doeg Settle on the score of alliteration :

With new-borne sighes and denisen'd [5] wit do sing;
You take wrong wayes; those far-fet helps be such
As do bewray a want of inward tuch,[6] touch [far-fetch'd
And sure, at length stolne goods doe come to light :
But if, both for your loue and skill, your name
You seeke to nurse at fullest breasts of Fame,
Stella behold, and then begin to endite.

XVI.

'*Loue's pain.*'

IN nature, apt to like,[7] when I did see
  Beauties which were of many carrets fine, carats
My boiling sprites did thither then incline,

" He was too warm on picking words to dwell,
  But fagoted his notions as they fell,
  And if they rhymed and rattled, all was well."
(Ab. and Achit. pt. 2). Christie has no note hereon. Sidney himself is alliterative beyond what one would expect from these lines, as an observant reader will soon detect.

[5] Q 2, has 'deuised'; Q 1, 'disguised'; both errors. Denisened is = naturalized in English.

[6] Not perhaps = touch in musical technical sense, but as if kindled tinder or coal = fire. See note on Son. ix. l. 14.

[7] = I being by nature apt to like. Hence 'native,' not as usual 'Nature.'

And, Loue, I thought that I was full of thee :
But finding not those restlesse flames in mee,
Which others said did make their soules to pine,
I thought those babes of some pinne's hurt did whine,
By my soule [8] iudging what Loue's paine might be.
But while I thus [9] with this young lyon plaid,
Mine eyes—shall I say curst or blest?—beheld
Stella : now she is nam'd, neede more be said ?
In her sight I a lesson new haue speld ;
I now haue learnd loue right, and learnd euen so
As they that being poysoned poyson know.[1]

---

[8] 2 qu. and Bright MS. 'love.' As Love is an extraneous personified power (l. 4), and as it is other souls that pine with the pains of love, 'soul' is superior.

[9] I accept here Q 2. In A 1613 'fool' is inserted in parenthesis after 'I.' In A it is not, nor is 'young,' thus leaving the line imperfect.

[1] Both for neatness of wording and metre I have preferred Q 1 to Q 2 and A; 'doth' is superfluous, and the trochee poisond is unpleasant, especially when 'doth poison' follows :

'As they | that be | ĭng poi | sŏn'd poi | son know
As who | by being | poisŏn'd | doth poi | son know.'

Moreover, that Q 1 is the better seems to be borne out by l. 3, where 'soon' (Q 2 and A) is not so expressive of the effect of great beauty on a nature apt to like all things as is 'then.'

XVII.
'*Cupid offending.*'

HIS mother deere, Cupid offended late,
Because that Mars, growne ² slacker in her loue,
With pricking shot he did not throughly moue
To keepe the place ³ of their first louing state.
The boy refusde for feare of Marses hate,   Mars'
Who threatned stripes, if he his wrath did proue ; ⁴
But she, in chafe, him from her lap did shoue,
Brake bowe, brake shafts, while ⁵ Cupid weeping sate ;
Till that his grandame Nature, pittying it,
Of Stella's browes made him two better bowes,

² 2 qu. 'grew'—not English; the construction being not—that Mars 'grew' slacker; but—that Cupid did not move Mars, [now] 'grown' slacker (A).
³ 'pace' in Q 2 and A and A 1613. This seems justified by 'move' (l. 3). But in sense here used, a 'state' does not 'pace,' and in no sense otherwise than very measuredly; whereas the metaphorical use of the technical hawking term 'place' (Q 1), the height to which the falcon soars, is most common. Hence I adjudge 'pace' to have been an accidental error in MS. or type of Q 2 unwittingly perpetuated in A and A 1613, and so return upon Q 1 for 'place.'   ⁴ = as we say, try.
⁵ 2 qu. 'where.' 'While' is so superior to 'where,' that I take the latter to be an error. The interchange is not uncommon.

And in her eyes of arrowes infinit.
O how for ioy he leapes! O how he crowes!
And straight therewith, like wags new got to play,
Fals to shrewd turnes; and I was in his way.

XVIII.

'Bankrout.'

WITH what sharpe [6] checkes I in my selfe am shent
    When into Reason's audite I do goe,
And by iust 'counts my selfe a bankrout know
Of all those goods which heau'n to me hath lent;
Vnable quite to pay euen Nature's rent,
Which vnto it by birthright I do ow;
And, which is worse, no good excuse can showe,
But that my wealth I haue most idly spent!
My youth doth waste, my knowledge brings forth toyes;
My wit doth striue those passions to defende,
Which, for reward, spoile [7] it with vaine annoyes.

---

[6] Q 2 'strange.' The 'checkes' by which he in himself is 'shent' are the considerations below, as in ll. 9-12; but these, though they might be and would be 'sharpe' in one of Sidney's dispositions, could not in any way, to a man like him, be 'strange' (2 qu.). Perhaps the latter was a misreading for 'strong'; 'shent' = scolded or punished.   [7] = despoil.

I see, my course to lose my selfe doth bend ;
I see—and yet no greater sorrow take
Than that I lose no more for Stella's sake.

XIX.
' Words . . . vainely spent.'

ON Cupid's bowe how are my heart-strings bent,
    That see my wracke, and yet embrace the same !
When most I glory, then I feele most shame ;
I willing run, yet while I run repent ;
My best wits still their owne disgrace inuent :
My very inke turnes straight to Stella's name ;
And yet my words, as them my pen doth frame,
Auise [8] themselues that they are vainely spent :
For though she passe all things, yet what is all
That vnto me, who fare like him that both
Lookes to the skies, and in a ditch doth fall ?
O let me prop my mind, yet in his growth,

---

[8] = advise. In Q 1 'accuse.' 'Advise' (= auise or warn) and 'accuse' seem almost equal ; but as the fault is not so much in the words as in the speaker, 'auise' is better. We have the word later in Hausted's Rivall Friends (1632), 'Are you *avis'd* of that ?' (*bis*, act v. sc. 4).

And not in nature for best fruits [9] vnfit.
Scholler, saith Loue, bend hitherward your [1] wit.

XX.
'*My death's wound.*'

FLY, fly, my friends; I haue my death's wound, fly;
See there that boy, that murthring boy, I say,
Who, like a theefe hid in darke [2] bush doth ly,
Till bloudy bullet get him wrongfull pray.   .   prey
So, tyran he, no fitter place could spie,
Nor so faire [3] leuell in so secret stay,
As that sweet black which vailes the heav'nly eye;
There himselfe with his shot he [4] close doth lay.
Poore passenger, passe now thereby I did,

---

[9] The Bright MS. has 'witts,' but clearly by mistake. 'Wits' do not grow in a mind as something new, the produce of the mind; and the verb 'prop,' as one props an overladen branch fit by nature for best fruit, but unable in growth to support the weight, seems decisive.   [1] Q 1 and Bright MS. 'thy.'

[2] As the whole Sonnet plays on the darkness of Stella's eyes, no doubt 'dark' of A and A 1613 is the later change for 'a' of 2 qu.

[3] 2 qu. 'farre'—an error for 'faire' of A and A 1613. Cupid could get no such secret ambush, nor one where he could 'level' so fairly = take so fair or excellent point-blank aim.

[4] Q 2 and Bright MS. and A 1613: 'he himself,' Q 1 and A.

And staid, pleas'd with the prospect of the place,
While that black hue from me the bad guest hid :
But straight I saw motions of lightning⁵ grace ;
And then descried the glistrings of his dart :
But ere I could flie thence, it pierc'd my heart.

XXI.

' Aught so faire as Stella is.'

YOUR words, my friend (right healthfull caustiks), blame
My young mind marde, whom Loue doth windlas⁶ so ;
That mine owne writings, like bad seruants, show

---

⁵ Q 2, 'lightning's grace.' This is a strange phrase, but 'lightning grace' is not; and while there is a constant interchange in MSS. of 'then' and 'there' (Q 1 and Q 2), the former agrees better with 'straight' (l. 12) and 'morions.'

⁶ =catch or ensnare craftily or by indirect acts, or perhaps envelop in snaring cords. A windlass (not the machine) is a circuitous course (see Golding's Cæsar, in Richardson, *s.v.*), and to 'windlas' is to fetch a windlass or compass: and as such indirectness is generally taken, whether in words, hunting, or at bowls, or in anything else, for policy's sake and to ensnare or find out, the word is commonly used in passages involving these meanings. See Hamlet, act ii. sc. 1. Some examples, with the explanation of the word, are given in the Edinburgh Review, No. 187. It is a curious instance of the association of craft with indirect ways in the human mind, that the engine called a windlass, which by

My wits quicke in vaine thoughts, in vertue lame;
That Plato I read for nought but if he tame   unless
Such coltish yeeres;[7] that to my birth I owe
Nobler desires, least else that friendly foe,
Great expectation, weare a traine of shame:
For since mad March[8] great promise made of mee,
If now the May[9] of my yeeres much decline,
What can be hoped my haruest-time will be?

winding moves weights that could not be moved by the same force directly applied, is called in French *singe*, the crafty ape. It may be added, that though some of the Elizabethan spellings lead to the belief that they adopted the plausible etymology of wind-lace, to lace windingly, the verb is doubtless formed from the substantive, and that again is connected with 'windles.'

[7] In Q 2 'giers,' which, as=gears, can hardly be a variant reading, but=gyres, it might be right, and may have been made when or after 'windlas' was substituted for 'menace' of Q 1. But as 'yeeres' of Q 1 is returned to in A and A 1613, it is safer to adhere to it. See also note on Sonnet xxxvi. l. 2, golden (A) yielding (Q 1 and Q 2): and in Sonnet xcviii. l. 7, 'though gald' of later Arcadias, 'though gold,' A and A 1605, and 'thus held,' Q 1 and Q 2.

[8] The Misprint 'Mars,' Q 1 (but it is curious 'mad Mars' occurs in Sonnet lxxv.) led to 'promise made *to* me,' and the error of 'to' probably escaped notice in correcting for Q 2, but was altered to the right word 'of' in A.

[9] See note on next sonnet, l. 2.

Sure, you say well, 'Your wisedome's golden myne
Dig¹ deepe with Learning's spade.' Now tell me this—
Hath this world aught so faire as Stella is?

XXII.

'The Sunne . . . did her but kisse.'

IN highest way of heav'n the sunne did ride,
    Progressing then from faire Twinnes'² gold'n place,
Hauing no maske³ of clowds before his face,
But streaming⁴ forth of heate in his chiefe pride;
When some faire ladies, by hard promise tied,
On horsebacke met him in his furious race;
Yet each prepar'd with fannes' wel-shading grace
From that foe's wounds their tender skinnes to hide.
Stella alone with face vnarmèd marcht,

---

¹ 2 Q 'digs,' in error.
² Q 1, in error, inserts 'in' after 'Twinnes.'
³ I accept this for 'scarf' of A and A 1613, seeing that as he compares the Sun's face with the ladies' and Stella's, it is more fitting, and probably later.
⁴ I adopt this from Q 1 in preference to 'shining' of Q 2, A, and A 1613, as more forcible.

Either to do like him which open [5] shone,
Or carelesse of the wealth, because her owne.
Yet were the hid and meaner beauties parcht;
Her dainties [6] bare went free : the cause was this,—
The sunne, that [7] others burn'd, did her but kisse.

XXIII.

'Pensivenesse.'

THE curious wits, seeing dull pensiuenesse
    Bewray it selfe in my long-settled eies,
Whence those same fumes of melancholy rise,
With idle paines and missing ayme, do guesse.
Some, that know how my spring I did addresse,
Deem [8] that my Muse some fruit of knowledge plies;

---

[5] Q 1 reads, not happily, 'as carelesse showne.'

[6] Q 2, by 'dainties' corrects the error of 'daintiest' in Q 1, A, A 1613, &c.

[7] I accept 'that' of Q 1, as better than 'which' of Q 2, A, and A 1613. With reference to this Sonnet, it is probable that in l. 10 of the preceding, there was an intended double conceit, and that it was written in May. The present one was evidently so written, or shortly after May. We may here recall Spenser's brilliant picture of May:

    'Then came fair May, the fayrest mayd on ground,' &c.

[8] Q 2, misreads 'deem'd.'

ASTROPHEL AND STELLA. 35

Others, because the prince my seruice tries,
Thinke that I thinke State errours to redress :
But harder iudges iudge ambition's [9] rage—
Scourge of it selfe, still climing slipperie place—
Holds my young braine captiv'd [1] in golden cage.
O fooles, or ouer-wise : alas, the race [2]

---

[9] More poetic and Elizabethan than 'ambitious' of 2 qu.

[1] Cf. Southwell (F. W. L. edn. s. v.)

[2] Query—have 'case'? But I doubt whether any example of case=cause, can be found. The converse error is made by 2 qu. lxiv. l. 7, of 'race' for 'case,' where ll. 2, 3, 6, 7 rhyme together, and where, therefore, l. 7 cannot repeat the 'race of' l. 2, such repetition being unknown in these sonnets. Besides, the words 'stop' and 'start' seem imperative for 'race '—the quick progress that sees nothing but the goal ; and this is confirmed by two parallel passages in the Countess of Pembroke's portion of the Psalms, e.g.

'While circling time, still ending and beginning,
Shall run the race when stop nor start appeares.'
Ps. lxxxix. st. x. ll. 1, 2.
'Thou makest the sunne the chariot-man of light
Well knowe the start and stop of dayly race.'
Ps. civ. st. ix. ll. 3, 4.

'Race' is used similarly in Sonnet xxii. l. 6 ; Sonnet xxvi. l. 13 (A), where it or 'case ' (2 qu.) may be taken, but where 'race ' seems better and more Sidneian ; Sonnet lx. l. 5, ' Fortune's race': Sonnet lxiv. l. 2, where the ' race ' of the passions is spoken of instead of his thoughts ; and, strangest use of all, Sonnet cv. l. 6,

Of all my thoughts hath³ neither stop nor start
But only Stella's eyes and Stella's hart.

XXIV.

' Rich, more wretched.'

RICH fooles there be whose base and filthie heart
    Lies hatching still the goods wherein they flow,
And damning their owne selues to Tantal's⁴ smart,
Wealth breeding want—more rich,⁵ more wretched
    growe :

—on which see our note,—' the telescope's dazzling race.' May not most of these passages be quoted as strengthening the original reading of King John (act iii. sc. 3), ' into the drowsy race of night' ?

³ 2 qu. read ' have.' As ' race of all my thoughts ' may mean the race of each of various thoughts, one striving against the other, the plural verb might be justified; but having the choice between it and ' hath ' (A and A 1613), we adopt the latter. Unless 'have' were determined in the plural by the accident of ' thoughts ' coming just before it, it would go also to prove ' race ' to be the true reading (as above) in l. 12, for ' case ' could not take a verb plural.

⁴ Q 1 has 'Tantalus his '—probably a corrector's attempt to amend some error in his copy, for the genetival form ' Tantalus his' is not found elsewhere in A & S.

⁵ So in 2 qu. and preferable to ' blest' of A and A 1613, seeing the whole sonnet is a sarcastic play on the name of Lord ' Rich.' See our Essay.

Yet to those fooles Heav'n doth such wit impart,
As what their hands do hold, their heads do know,
And knowing loue, and louing lay apart
As sacred things, far from all danger's show.[6]
But that rich foole, who by blind Fortune's lot
The richest gemme of loue and life enioyes,
And can with foule abuse such beauties blot;
Let him, depriu'd of sweet but vnfelt ioyes,
Exild for ay from those high treasures which
He knowes not, grow in only folly rich!

XXV.

'*Vertue . . . takes Stella's shape.*'

THE wisest scholler of the wight most wise[7]
By Phœbus' doome, with sugred sentence sayes,

---

[6] This has been hitherto punctuated into puzzling nonsense. I have re-punctuated so as to bring out the sense = 'and knowing [what their hands hold], they lay love and loving apart (as they would sacred things) far from even the show of danger.' 'Scattered' of Q 2 is a misreading of 'sacred.'

[7] I have deleted comma (,) after 'wise' as obscuring the sense. Socrates was pronounced by the oracle 'the wisest of men': Plato, his scholar, spoke as in text.

That vertue, if it once met[8] with our eyes,
Strange flames of loue it in our soules would raise;
But,—for that man with paine this truth descries, because
Whiles[9] he each thing in Sense's ballance wayes,
And so nor will nor can behold those skies
Which inward sunne[1] to heroick minde displaies—
Vertue of late, with vertuous care to ster   stir
Loue of herselfe,[2] tooke Stella's shape, that she
To mortall eyes might sweetly shine in her.
It is most true; for since I her did see,
Vertue's great beauty in that[3] face I proue,
And find th' effect,[4] for I do burne in loue.

[8] 2 qu. misread 'meete'=if it once did meet. So in l. 10 the past tense is required.

[9] =during the time when, more substantial than 'while' (Q 1 and Q 2), and hence 'whiles' better here.

[1] 2 qu. misread 'summe.'

[2] 2 qu. here and throughout read 'himself.' Virtue (ἀρετή, virtus) is always personified as a female (even *virtus*, manly valour), and there is no necessity here for changing the sex. Cf. also Son. ix. 'Queen Virtue.'

[3] 2 qu. 'her.' The 'her' may have come from 'her' just above, or may have been the Author's; but strictly speaking, 'that face' (A and A 1613) is more correct, seeing it was not Stella's face only, but *ex supp*. Virtue's and Stella's. It is Virtue's great beauty that he sees. See longer Notes and Illustrations, (*b*) at close for more.

[4] Q 1 has 'defect'—a curious instance of error from sound.

XXVI.

'Astrologic.'

THOUGH dustie[5] wits dare scorne Astrologie,
And fooles can thinke those lampes of purest light—
Whose numbers, waies,[6] greatnesse, eternity,
Promising wonders, wonder do inuite[7]—
To haue for no cause birthright in the sky[8]
But for to spangle the blacke weeds of Night;
Or for some braule, which in that chamber hie,
They should still daunce to please a gazer's sight.
For me, I do Nature vnidle[9] know,
And know great causes great effects procure;
And know those bodies high raigne on the low.
And if these rules did faile, proofe makes me sure,

---

[5] Better than 'duskie' of Q 1 and Q 2, as = earth-lord.

[6] = ways, not 'weighs.'

[7] 2 qu. read "Promising wondrous wonders to inuite." There seems no sense in this, while A is clear, which says—whose numbers, ways, &c., as they promise wonders to the inquirer, so do they invite wonder.

[8] 2 qu. 'skyes'—error. Cf. rhymes 'eternitie,' l. 3, and 'hie,' l. 7.

[9] Here and elsewhere 'idle' does not mean wholly passive or resting, but frivolously or triflingly employed. Cf. 'idle toys.'

Who oft fore-see[1] my after-following race,[2]
By only those two starres in Stella's face.

XXVII.

'Most alone in greatest company.'

BECAUSE I oft in darke abstracted guise
   Seeme most alone in greatest company,
With dearth of words, or[3] answers quite awrie,
To them that would make speech of speech arise;
They deeme, and of their doome the rumour flies,
That poison foule of bubbling pride doth lie
So in my swelling breast, that only I
Fawne on my selfe, and[4] others do despise.

---

[1] I adopt this from Q 2, as more accurate than 'fore-iudge' (by the stars). Q 1 has 'bewraies.'

[2] See note on xxiii. l. 12. Looking well to it in itself and to the other examples quoted, while probably Sidney did write 'case' here as in Q 1 and Q 2, I think on revision he changed it to 'fore-see .... race,' in the sense of progress of events. Thus taken it seems more poetic, and the sense more comprehensive.

[3] 2 qu. 'and.'

[4] 2 qu. 'all.' This is more taking, but it makes an ambiguous sentence (=it might be myself [whom] all others do despise—a meaning not the Author's; and by ' ⏑ ' instead of ' ⏑ ' the rhythm is worsened.

Yet pride I thinke doth not my soule possesse
(Which looks too oft in his⁵ vnflattering glasse) : ♂
But one worse fault, ambition, I confesse,
That makes me oft my best friends ouerpasse,
Vnseene, vnheard, while thought to highest place⁶
Bends all his powers, euen vnto Stella's grace.

XXVIII.

'*Allegorie.*'

YOU that with Allegorie's curious frame
Of others' children changelings vse to make,
With me those paines, for God's sake,⁷ do not take
I list not dig so deepe for brasen fame.
When I say⁸ Stella, I doe meane the same
Princesse of beauty, for whose only sake

---

⁵ Q 1 and Q 2, 'this.' The soul looks in 'his vnflattering glasse;' but it is difficult to see how he could look in 'this,' because there is nothing to which 'this' can refer. A common misinterchange.

⁶ See note on Sonnet xvii. l. 4.

⁷ Q 2, 'good now' seems an attempt to soften down 'God's sake' (Q 1) to which A and A 1613 return.

⁸ 2 qu. 'see'—an evident error.

The raines of Loue I loue, though neuer slake,[9] slack
And ioy therein, though Nations count it shame.
I beg no subiect to vse eloquence,
Nor in hid wayes do[1] guide philosophie;
Looke at my hands for no such quintessence;
But know that I in pure simplicitie
Breathe out the flames which burne within my heart,
Loue onely reading[2] unto me this arte.

XXIX.

'Given vp for a slaue.'

LIKE some weak lords neighbord by mighty kings,
To keep themselues and their chiefe cities free,

---

[9] = though the reins are never slack, and by their tight curbing pain me.

[1] 2 qu. 'to' Either might be with Q 2 and A reading, but Q 1 reading 'hidden ways' rather requires 'do,' yet has 'to.' Hence, as frequently, we may take this as an error which escaped correction in the altered copy of Q 1, from which Q 2 was printed; fetched probably from 'to' of line above.

[2] Looking to the arts of eloquence (l. 9) and philosophy (l. 10), which were in technical language 'read' in the Schools, I prefer the probably after-change 'reading' (A and A 1613), and 'unto' to 'leading' . . . 'into' (Q 1 and Q 2).

Do easly yeeld that all their coasts³ may be
Ready to store⁴ their campes of needfull things;
So Stella's heart, finding what power Loue brings,
To keep it selfe in life and liberty,
Doth willing graunt that in the frontiers⁵ he
Vse all to helpe his other conquerings.
And thus her heart escapes; but thus her eyes
Serue him with shot, her lips his heralds are,
Her breasts his tents, legs his triumphall carre,⁶
Her flesh⁷ his food, her skin his armour braue;
And I, but for because my prospect lies   only
Vpon that coast, am giv'n vp for a⁸ slaue.

---

³ (A) is more correct, as more than one lord and one kingdom is spoken of; besides, the plural was often used in this sense, even when one kingdom or province was spoken of; witness our English Bible : *e.g.* 'all the *coasts* of Egypt,' Exodus x. 14; 'all thy *coasts*,' Deut. xxviii. 40. So that 'coast' of Q 1 and Q 2 is an error.

⁴ 2 qu. 'serve.' One 'serves' a meal or a guest, but 'stores' (A) a camp; and 'stores' is also the stronger.

⁵ 2 qu. 'frontire.' Either might be adopted; but as he enumerates different frontiers below (see note on line 2) 'frontiers' (A) is adhered to.

⁶ 2 qu. 'chare,' old form of 'car.'

⁷ 2 qu. 'selfe '—a mistake, of which there are several examples in Donne, for 'flesh.'   ⁸ Omitted in 2 qu.

XXX.

'Questions.'

WHETHER the Turkish new moone minded be
    To fill her[9] hornes this yeere on Christian coast?
How Poles'[1] right king means without leaue of hoast
To warme with ill-made fire cold Muscouy?   [host
If French can yet three parts in one agree?
What now the Dutch in their full diets boast?
How Holland hearts, now so good townes be[2] lost,

---

[9] The Author, thinking rather of the Turk, has 'his' (A and A 1613); but 'her' (2 qu.) is more correct, and I adopt it. In like manner Shakespeare and the author of Cock Lorell's Bote call Hesperus 'her,' because to English Latinate ears Venus was the common and more personal name.

[1] 2 qu. 'Poland's king.' The Polish monarchy was elective, and when the foreigner, Henry of Valois, left the throne of Poland to take that of France, the nobles elected Stephen Bathori, a Pole (1575). Hence 'the Poles' right king' of A and A 1613. Both, however, were probably written by Sidney, for the after-change of A was not a prudent phrase in 1581, when 'Monsieur' came over to woo Elizabeth, and when Sidney had already been outspoken beyond what seemed prudent, and could only await results. There seems no doubt that, directly or indirectly, Sidney himself was offered the throne of Poland.

[2] 2 qu. 'are.' English idiom allows 'be,' and with good effect.

Trust in the shade of pleasant³ Orange-tree?
How Vlster likes of that same⁴ golden bit
Wherewith my father once made it halfe tame?
If in the Scotch Court be no weltring⁵ yet?
These questions busie wits to me do frame:
I, cumbred with good maners, answer doe,
But know not how; for still I thinke of⁶ you.

XXXI.
'The Moone.'

WITH how sad steps, O Moone, thou clim'st the skies!
How silently, and with how wanne⁷ a face!

---

³ 2 qu. 'pleasing '—but 'pleasant ' (A and Λ 1613) the better epithet for a tree.

⁴ 2 qu. 'the same.' Sidney's father's successes were remarkable, and never more so than on the third occasion of his being sent over; and 'that' seems to call attention to this, and to be stronger, and therefore preferable.

⁵ '*No weltering*' is stronger and more expressive of the turbulence and broils of the Scotch Court. Hence I prefer A and A 1613 to 2 qu. 'If in the Scottish Court be weltering yet.'

⁶ 2 qu. 'on': 'of' is a favourite particle with Sidney, and to 'think *of*' is stronger and more expressive of full-given thought than 'on.'

⁷ So, in A, 'wan '; but in 2 qu. and other Arcadia texts

What, may it be that euen in heau'nly place
That busie archer his sharpe arrowes tries!
Sure, if that long-with-loue-acquainted eyes
Can iudge of loue, thou feel'st a louer's case,
I reade it in thy lookes ; thy languisht grace,
To me, that feele the like, thy state discries.[8]

'meane.' With our present sense 'meane' is intolerable; but in Sidney's time it may have been an adjectival use of mean or mene = lamenting. See note on Sonnet xxxv. l. 11.

[8] ll. 7, 8. These lines, according to reading and punctuation of 2 qu.—viz.

'I reade within thy lookes thy languisht grace,
To mee that feele the like, my state descries :'

—form each a clause. But though one reads 'in' out of or through, to read a thing within one's looks is a strange phrase and it is difficult, if not impossible, to understand how one can read an outward and visible sign like the moon's languisht grace, i. e., her 'wan face' of l. 2, 'within her looks.' Again, if l. 8 be a distinct clause, the state descries—what? The rhythm too agrees in making 'looks' end one clause, and 'descries' the other. But if so, 'I read within thy looks' is not sense, whereas 'I read it in thy looks' (A and A 1613) is. And again, in the next clause, the construction is, To me that feel the like (my sympathy giving me the insight) thy languisht grace, thy wan (pale) face, descries = points out 'thy' state. Since, therefore, O Moon, I have rightly divined your state, then of fellowship tell me, &c. 'My' is clearly one of those frequent pronominal interchanges that transcribers make unwittingly, or to give a fancied sense of

Then, eu'n of fellowship, O Moone, tell me,
Is constant loue deem'd there but want of wit?
Are beauties there as proud as here they[9] be?
Do they aboue loue to be lou'd, and yet

their own. It would be absurd of the Moon to point out to Sidney his own state. 'Descries' is now used in the reflective sense of pointing out to oneself, or rather perhaps in the sense of seeing out or beyond; but in Sidney's day it had also the meaning of pointing out to another, as here and as in the Countess of Pembroke's Passion (Stanza lxxvi.) :
'Behould the heavens what sorrowe they did showe,
And how the earth her dolor did *discrye*'
We have 'descry' used thus much later, *e. g.* in Lod. Barrey's 'Ram Alley' (1636), as follows:
'some scullion in a hole
Begot thee on a gipsie, or
Thy mother was some Collier's whore;
"My rampant tricks!" you rogue, thou't be descride
Before our plot be ended.
W. S. What should *descry* him,
Vnless it be his nose?" Act ii. sc. 1.
The 'nose' is after the type of Bardolph's, and could not fail to 'point out' its owner. See also Stanza viii. l. 2, and Psalms cxix M. l. 3.

[9] This is more indefinite and therefore better than 'there' (2 qu). 'There' implies that there are others in the world not proud; but in his love Stella is all the world and all womankind to him, and so is she in his bitterness and despair. That the correct reading is 'they' is also shown by 'they' of ll. 12 and 14.

Those louers scorne whom that loue doth possesse?
Doe they call vertue there vngratefulnesse?

XXXII.

'Morpheus.'

MORPHEUS, the liuely[1] sonne of deadly Sleepe,
Witnesse of life to them that liuing die,
A prophet oft, and oft an historie,[2]
A poet eke, as humours fly or[3] creepe;
Since thou in me so sure a power doest keepe,
That neuer I with clos'd-vp sense do lie,
But by thy worke my Stella I discrie,
Teaching blind eyes both how to smile and weepe;
Vouchsafe, of all acquaintance, this to tell,
Whence hast thou iuorie, rubies, pearle, and gold,
To shew her skin, lips, teeth, and head so well?
Foole! answers he; no Indes such treasures hold;
But from thy heart, while my sire[4] charmeth thee,
Sweet Stella's image I do steale to mee.

---

[1] = life-like or motioning.
[2] This line is curiously perverted in the borrowing by Griffin (*Fidessa* Son. xv). 'A Comedie it is, and now an Historie.'
[3] 2 qu. 'and'—a mistake.
[4] = Somnus or Morpheus (l. 1). 'Fire,' a modern error, as in Gray, &c. It is 'Sire' in 2 qu. and A 1613, &c.

XXXIII.

' I might.'

I MIGHT !—vnhappie word—O me, I might,
    And then would not, or[5] could not, see my blisse;
Till now wrapt in a most infernall night,
I finde how heau'nly day, wretch ! I did[6] misse.
Hart, rent thy selfe, thou dost thy selfe but right;
No louely Paris made thy Hellen his;
No force, no fraud robd thee of thy delight,
Nor Fortune of thy fortune author is;
But to my selfe my selfe did giue the blow,
While too much wit, forsooth, so troubled me,
That I respects for both our sakes must show :
And yet could not, by rysing morne fore-see
How faire a day was neare : O punisht eyes,
That I had bene more foolish, or more wise !

---

[5] 2 qu. 'nor,' but 'or' gives the better sense, because Sidney represents himself as doubtful of which might be the reason.
[6] Better than 'did I' of 2 qu. from A and A 1613.

XXXIV.

' How can words ease?'

COME, let me write.⁷ And to what end? To ease
A burthened hart. How can words ease, which are
The glasses of thy dayly-vexing care?
Oft cruell fights well pictured-forth do please.
Art not asham'd to publish thy disease?
Nay, that may breed my fame, it is so rare.
But will not wise men thinke thy words fond ware?
Then be they close, and so none shall displease.⁸

---

⁷ There are propositions and questioning answers here between his passion wit and his more essential or intellectual wit. 1st Wit says, 'Come, let me write.' 2d Wit, 'To what end?' (1st) 'To ease .... heart'; (2d) 'How .... care' (1st) 'Oft ... please,' l. 4; (2d) l. 5; (1st) l. 6; (2d) l. 7; (1st) l. 8; (2d) l. 9; (1st) l. 10; (2d) l. 11. I have made the punctuation—hitherto mere confusion—accord herewith. So throughout.

⁸ 2 qu. read, 'Then be they close, and they shall none displease.' Cf. our text (A and A 1613). Both readings will suit, but A is the later; probably for this reason 2d Wit objects what 'wise men' will think. 1st Wit answers according to 2 qu. that if kept close none will be displeased; and Sidney seeing this makes him solicitous as to whether he displeases fools as well as wise—the multitude as well as the few—seems to have altered it to make 'none' a nominative agreeing with 'words.' The construction, however, is

What idler thing then speake and not be hard?[9] than
What harder thing then smart and not to speake ?
Peace, foolish wit ! with wit my wit is mard.
Thus write I, while I doubt to write, and wreake
My harmes in ink's poore losse. Perhaps some find
Stella's great powrs, that so confuse my mind.

XXXV.
'*Grow rich, meaning my Stella's name.*'

WHAT may words say, or what may words not say,
Where Truth it selfe must speake like Flatterie ?
Within what bounds can one his liking stay,
Where Nature doth with infinite agree ?
What Nestor's counsell can my flames alay,
Since Reason's selfe doth blow the coale in[10] me ?

---

awkward. Indeed, after all, 'none' may be=not at all, and in such case 2 qu. offer the better reading.

[9] hard=heard.

[10] 2 qu. 'to.' As he speaks of 'his flames,' and as the coal is the love within him, and as he means his inward Reason itself increases the flame of love 'in' him, 'in' (A and A 1613) seems preferable, and so 'coale' (*ib.*) as generic rather than 'coals' (Q 1 and Q 2). This was a proverbial expression at and before the time Sidney wrote :—

" For lowly life withstandeth envy quite,
As floating ship, by bearing sail a low,
Withstandeth storms, when boisterous winds do blow,

And, ah, what hope that Hope should once see day,
Where Cupid is sworne page to Chastity?
Honour is honour'd, that thou doest possesse
Him as thy slaue, and now long-needy Fame
Doth euen grow rich,[1] meaning[2] my Stella's name.
Wit learnes in thee perfection to expresse,
Not thou by praise, but praise in thee is raisde :
It is a praise to praise, when thou art praisde.

>   Thy usage thus, in time shall win the goal.
>   Though doubtful haps, dame Fortune sends between ;
>   And thou shalt see thine enemies *blow the coal:*"
>   TUSSER, (1812 Rp. p. 312.)

[1] Another play on 'Rich'—Stella being Lady Rich. So Henry Constable's Diana, Son. x. and Addl. Son. vi. p. 39.

[2] I adopt this from 2 qu. in preference to 'naming.' Pinkerton has stated that 'mean' is still used in Scottish law phraseology as 'declaring,' or as we would say, setting forth ; and it has been well remarked that in Midsummer-Night's Dream Shakespeare seems by the use of 'videlicet' to be using a law term in a burlesque sense :

> 'And thus she [Thisbe] means, videlicet.'

The present phrase of 'Fame *meaning*,' *i.e.* declaring or setting forth Stella's name, may be taken as the decisive phrase that was wanting to confirm this view. Only it must be added that Shakespeare probably made Demetrius pun, and use the word in the double sense of 'set forth' her case, and mean, moan or lament. For the later sense see our note on Sonnet xxxi. l. 2.

XXXVI.

' New assaults.'

STELLA, whence doth these new assaults arise,
A conquerd yeelding³ ransackt heart to winne,
Whereto long since, through my long-battred eyes,
Whole armies of thy beauties entred in ?
And there, long since, Loue, thy lieuetenant, lies ;
My forces razde,⁴ thy banners raisd within :⁵

---

³ I adopt this from 2 qu., as 'golden' of A and A 1613 seems to be the same kind of mistake as 'giers' for 'years' (Q 1 and A) in Sonnet xxi. l. 6.   Cf. also 'this held' (Q 1 and Q 2) for 'though gald,' later A: Sonnet xcviii. l. 7.

⁴ = erased from the muster-roll, the word being chosen for its similarity in sound to 'rais'd.' But had not the readings been unanimous, I should have queried 'forces' as against 'fortress.'

⁵ All the editions agree in [.] after 'in' (l. 4), but 2 qu. have no stop after 'within' (l. 6) = thy banners of conquest, while A punctuates within : = effects of conquest. A continuation of the clause into the first part of the next line is frequent in these sonnets, and the 'what' of 2 qu. (l. 7) favours the view that Sidney meant banners of conquest, and the plural 'assaults' (l. 1) and 'new' (l. 8) seem to approve their readings of this sonnet. Accordingly I accept 'these assaults ' for 'this assault' (A and A 1613): 'doth' = from what 'doth' arrive these new assaults. I read in l. 7 'do not,' else there would be for these sonnets the unusual foot | Of conquest | , and besides, without 'not' (as in Q 1 and Q 2) the clause is meaningless.

Of conquest do not these effects suffice,
But wilt new warre vpon thine owne begin?
With so sweet voyce, and by sweet Nature so[6]
In sweetest strength, so sweetly skild withal
In all sweet stratagems sweete Art can show,[7]
That not my soule, which at thy foot did fall
Long since, forc'd by thy beames: but[8] stone nor tree,
By Sence's priuiledge, can scape from thee!

XXXVII.[9]

' No misfortune but that Rich she is.'

MY mouth doth water, and my breast doth swell,
    My tongue doth itch, my thoughts in labour be:

---

[6] The sense is at first sight obscure. The construction is, with so sweet voice and by sweet Nature [formed] so [*i.e.* so sweet] in sweetest strength. On the supposition that there is an ellipse, ' and by sweet Nature [formed] so [sweet] in sweetest strength ' we have tautology, albeit not uncharacteristic lingering over ' sweet.'

[7] The punctuation has been hitherto ruined by the lavish use of commas. ' With .... strength' is a clause telling what Nature did: ' so sweetly .... show' is the clause telling what Art has done. I have punctuated accordingly.

[8] This is supposed to contain the negative expressed above and afterwards, and to be equal to ' but not' or ' but now.'

[9] See our Essay on this Sonnet.

Listen then, lordings, with good eare to me,
For of my life I must a riddle tell.
Towárd Aurora's Court a nymph doth dwell,
Rich in all beauties which man's eye can see ;
Beauties so farre from reach of words, that we
Abase her praise saying she doth excell ;
Rich in the treasure of deserv'd renowne,
Rich in the riches of a royall hart,
Rich in those gifts which giue th' eternall crowne ;
Who, though most rich in these and euery part
Which make the patents of true worldly blisse,
Hath no misfortune but that Rich she is.

XXXVIII.

'The unkinde guest.'

THIS night, while sleepe begins with heauy wings
    To hatch[1] mine eyes, and that vnbitted thought
Doth fall to stray, and my chiefe powres are brought

---

[1] =shut or close—it is 'close' in 2 qu. For 'that' (A and A 1613) 2 qu. read ' the '—the former far better=while that, because it separates ' his thought ' from the extraneous power 'sleep,' while ' the ' rather connects them. Cf. also ' my chief powres,' which is also against 'the.'

To leaue the scepter of all subiect things;
The first that straight my fancie's errour brings
Vnto my mind is Stella's image, wrought
By Loue's owne selfe, but with so curious drought
That she, methinks, not onely shines but sings.
I start, looke, hearke; but what in closde-vp sence[2]
Was held, in opend[3] sense it flies away,
Leauing me nought but wayling eloquence.
I, seeing better sights in sight's[4] decay,
Cald[5] it anew,[6] and wooèd Sleepe againe;
But him, her host, that vnkind guest had slaine.

---

[2] = was held in the closed-up senses.   2 qu. misread 'inclos'd-up,' which is not English; nor does it give sense in this passage.

[3] 2 qu. 'open': the former almost demanded by 'clos'd'; and Sidney is speaking of awakened, *i. e.* opened sense, not of open sense. There are at least seven instances of the omission of a final *d* in the transcript of these poems, and several where *d* has been wrongly added.

[4] 2 qu. 'sighes'—the latter a mistake. He says that in sight's decay, *i.e.* in sleep, he sees better sights, that is, Stella's image, than when awake.

[5] '*conclude* anew,' Q 2. Probably variations like 'close' and 'hatch'; but 'conclude' = shut up [my lids] is strange and harsh, and so probably thought Sidney after the novelty of the change was over, for A (as A 1613), which in this sonnet agrees everywhere else with Q 2 against Q 1, here returns to the reading of the latter, 'Cald.'   [6] Q 2, 'a new'—only one of the old ways of writing 'anew,' like 'a bed' for 'abed.'

XXXIX.

'*Sleepe.*'

COME, Sleepe! O Sleepe, the certaine knot of peace,
The baiting-place[7] of wit, the balme of woe,
The poore man's wealth, the prisoner's release,
Th'[8] indifferent iudge betweene the high and low;
With shield[9] of proofe shield me from out the prease
Of those[1] fierce darts Despaire at me doth throw:
O make in me those ciuill warres to cease;
I will good tribute pay, if thou do so.
Take thou of me smooth pillowes, sweetest bed,
A chamber deafe of noise and blind of[2] light,

---

[7] 2 qu. erroneously read 'bathing'; =refreshing place. See our Essay on this whole Sonnet. For 'wit,' 2 qu. read 'wits' = witty men.

[8] The variations 'Th'' 'The,' are mere scribes' carelessnesses.

[9] One man, and Sleep is one, and is represented as single throughout ll. 1-4, carries one shield (A and A 1613): hence 'shields' of 2 qu. incorrect.

[1] 2 qu. 'these'; but 'those' more agrees with the sense, and is required by 'those civil wars,' l. 7.

[2] I take 'of' as more Sidnean, from Q 1 and Q 2, and think 'to .... to,' the Countess's or Editor's improvements. So too 'in' (l. 12) for 'by.'

A rosie garland[3] and a weary hed:
And if these things, as being thine in right,
Moue not thy heauy grace, thou shalt in me,
Liuelier then else-where, Stella's image[4] see.

XL.

' Nowe of the basest.'

AS good to write, as for to lie and grone.
  O Stella deare, how much thy power hath wrought,
That[5] hast my mind—nowe[6] of the basest—brought

---

[3] '*rosie garland*,' as the garland of silence (*sub rosa*)—a pun that would have delighted Thomas Fuller, and Charles Lamb if he had noticed it. For a curious instance of the same use of 'rose' for 'silence,' see H. S's address prefixed to the Arcadia, given in its place in the second portion of the present Volume.

[4] Q 1 has 'rare Stella's'—an early reading, altered probably because it required an awkward elision, Stella's image.

[5] So our text (A 1613), in agreement with 2 qu. A has 'Thou.' I accept 'That.'

[6] 'none' in our text (A 1613), in agreement with A; but in 2 qu. there is the very remarkable reading of ' nowe,' which I adopt. Granted that 'w' is a common error for 'n'; granted also that a mind may be wrecked while becoming base is quite a different thing. But is not this 'different thing' just what we long for a recognition of by Sidney in the conditions under which these

My still-kept course, while others sleepe, to mone;
Alas, if from the height of Vertue's throne
Thou canst vouchsafe the influence of a thought
Vpon a wretch that long thy grace hath sought,
Weigh then how I by thee am ouerthrowne;
And then thinke thus—although thy beautie be
Made manifest by such a victorie,
Yet noble[7] conquerours do wreckes[8] auoid.
Since then thou hast so farre subduèd me,
That in my heart I offer still to thee,
O do not let thy temple be destroyd.

Sonnets were composed? Is 'nowe' not that sharp cry of mingled penitence and fascination one would wish to hear? See more of this in our Essay.

[7] I accept 'noble' from A in preference to 'noblest' of 2 qu. and A 1613 := conquerors at all entitled to the epithet 'noble.'

[8] Q 1, 'wreakes': Q 2 'wreake': 'wrecks,' A: 'wreckes,' A 1613. Q 1 and A and A 1613 agree in s. There is in this sonnet no question of Stella revenging herself or having cause for revenge; but he speaks in previous lines of the 'wreck' he is becoming, and (in l. 14) asks her not to destroy that which is her temple, viz. himself. Perhaps one of the most noticeable of these sonnets autobiographically.

XLI.

'Stella lookt on.'

HAUING this day my horse, my hand, my launce
    Guided so well that I obtain'd the prize,
Both by the iudgement of the English eyes
And of some sent from that sweet enemy Fraunce;
Horsemen my skill in horsemanship advaunce,
Towne folkes my strength; a daintier iudge applies
His praise to sleight which from good vse doth rise;
Some luckie wits impute it but to chance;
Others, because of[9] both sides I doe take
My blood from them who did excell in this,
Thinke Nature me a man-at-armes[1] did make.
How farre they shot awrie! the true cause is,
Stella lookt on, and from her heau'nly face
Sent forth the beames which made so faire my[2] race.

---

[9] '*of*' (A and A 1613) implies, and in that day still more implied, relationship, as in offspring; besides, the double 'from' (Q 1 and Q 2) is awkward; '*from* both sides he took his blood *from* them.'

[1] I take 'at' (Q 1 and Q 2) rather than 'of' (A and A 1613), because 'at' is our present form, and both were then used.

[2] '*my*' (A and A 1613)—superior to 'a' (Q 1 and Q 2).

XLII.

'Eyes.'

O EYES, which doe the spheares of beautie moue ;
Whose beames be³ ioyes, whose ioyes all vertues be ;
Who, while they make Loue conquer, conquer Loue ;
The schooles where Venus hath learn'd chastitie :
O eyes, where humble lookes most glorious proue,
Onely-lov'd tyrans,⁴ iust in cruelty ;—
Do not, O doe not, from poore me remoue,⁵
Keep still my zenith, euer shine on me :
For though I neuer see them, but straightwayes
My life forgets to nourish languisht sprites ;
Yet still on me, O eyes, dart downe your rayes :
And if from maiestie of sacred lights
Oppressing mortall sense my death proceed,
Wrackes triumphs be⁶ which Loue hie set doth breed.

³ Q 1 and Q 2 'all'—at first an attractive reading : but if the 'beames' be 'all' joys, then the joys cannot be all virtues, or virtuous.

⁴ So in A, and accepted. It is to be noted that in A, where the spelling, on the whole, has been carefully attended to, 'tyrant' is invariably, as in Ben Jonson, and in agreement with its derivation, 'tyran,' and plural 'tyrans.' We may take this therefore to have been Sidney's own spelling.

⁵ 2 qu. delete 'O,' and insert 'one' before 'remove.'

⁶ 2 qu. read stupidly 'best.'

XLIII.

' Leaue to die.'

FAIRE eyes, sweet lips, deare heart, that foolish I
    Could hope, by Cupid's helpe, on you to pray,
Since to himselfe he doth your gifts apply,
As his maine force, choise[7] sport, and easefull stay!
For when he will see who dare him gain-say,
Then with those eyes he lookes : lo, by and by
Each soule dothe at Loue's feet his weapons lay,
Glad if for her he giue them leaue to die.
When he will play, then in her lips he is,
Where blushing red, that Loue's selfe them doth [8] loue,
With either lip he doth the other kisse ;
But when he will, for quiet's sake, remoue
From all the world, her hart is then his rome,
Where well he knowes no man to him can come.

---

[7] 2 qu. 'chief'—a third instance of this change, showing it to be intentional. See Sonnet lx. l. 2.

[8] 2 qu. 'doe.' As in Donne and other MSS., there is a constant yet inconstant interchange of 'doth' and 'doe.' A and A 1613 almost always correct in this.

XLIV.

' Inward smart.'

MY words I know do well set forth my minde ;
My mind bemones his sense of inward smart ;
Such smart may pitie claime of any hart ;
Her heart, sweet heart, is of no tygre's kind :
And yet[9] she heares, and yet no pitie I find,
But more I cry, lesse grace she doth impart.
Alas, what cause is there so ouerthwart,[1]
That Noblenesse it selfe makes thus vnkind ?
I much do ghesse, yet finde no truth saue this,
That when the breath of my complaints[2] doth tuch
Those daintie dores vnto the Court of Blisse,
The heav'nly nature of that place is such,
That, once come there, the sobs of mine annoyes
Are metamorphos'd straight to tunes of ioyes.

---

[9] The repetition of 'and yet' is in the true mannerism of the time, and hence is preferable to 'And yet .... and,' it being understood that there is an elision at 'pitie' I.' Cf. Sonnet lvii. l. 5, &c. The 'yet' is used in double sense ; the first 'yet' being as often = 'still' or continually, the second = 'still' or up to this time.

[1] =opposite, cross.

[2] Better than 'complaint' of 2 qu. Cf. ll. 6, 13, 14.

XLV.

'*Imag'd things.*'

STELLA oft sees the very face of wo [3]
 Painted in my beclowded stormie face,
But cannot skill to pitie my disgrace,
Not though thereof the cause herself she know : [4]
Yet hearing late a fable, which did show
Of louers neuer knowne, a grieuous case,
Pitie thereof gate in her breast such place,
That, from that sea deriv'd, teares' spring did flow. [5]
Alas, if Fancie, drawne by imag'd things

---

[3] Better than 'woes' (2 qu.) as in a 'man of woe.'

[4] '*know :*' again better than 'knows,' as being more grammatically correct. Besides the 's' form does not rhyme, as it must do, with ll. 5-8, seeing there is no instance throughout these sonnets of there being more than two rhymes in the first eight lines. The 'No' of 2 qu. for 'not' is a mistake, due to the 't' of the next word, and A and A 1613 return to Q 1, reading 'Not.'

[5] In this sonnet Q 1 is clearly the earlier, and A and A 1613 change in l. 8 'That from that sea deriv'd tears spring did flow,' compared with the reading in the text (A and A 1613), decisively shows the latter to be the later, the new image being according to the then philosophy of the rise of springs by 'privie ways in the earth from the ocean.' See note in our SOUTHWELL, *s. v.*, and cf. DONNE, *s.v.*; also Browne's Brit. Pastorals, Mariner's Song (i. 2).

Though false, yet with free scope, more grace doth
  breed
Than seruants' wracke, where new doubts honor brings ;
Then thinke, my deare, that you in me[6] do reed
Of louers' ruine some thrise-sad[7] tragedie.
I am not I ; pitie the tale of me.

XLVI.

'*Blind-hitting Boy.*'

I CURST thee oft, I pitie now thy case,
  Blind-hitting Boy, since she that thee and me
Rules with a becke, so tyranniseth thee,
That thou must want or food or dwelling-place,
For she protests to banish thee her face :
Her face ! O Loue, a roge thou then shouldst be, rogue

---

[6] '*you in me*' (A and A 1613), not 'in me you' (2 qu.), is the later text and better, because an emphasis is thrown on the 'me,' which points out that he would be considered as the sad tragedy.

[7] I could not resist the temptation of the epithet here 'thrise' from Q 2. Against it is the earlier Q 1, and A and A 1613 return to the earlier. Still the very inevitable elongation in reading seems the more to tell of the 'sad tragedy.'

If Loue learne not alone to loue and see,
Without desire to feed of further grace.
Alas, poor wag, that now a scholler art
To such a schoolemistresse, whose lessons new
Thou needs must misse, and so thou needs must smart.
Yet, deare, let me his pardon get of you,
So long,[8] though he from book myche[9] to desire,
Till without fewell you[1] can make hot fire.

XLVII.
'Gaine to misse.'

WHAT, haue I thus betrayed my libertie !
    Can those blacke beames such burning markes engraue
In my free side; or am I borne a slaue,
Whose necke becomes such yoke of tyrannie !
Or want I sense to feele my miserie,

---

[8] He asks for Cupid's pardon until &c. There is no kind of pardon mentioned, and therefore 2 qu. are wrong in reading 'this pardon.'

[9] =to play truant: 'to miche' is a modern error not in A texts.

[1] 'Thou' of 2 qu. disagrees with 'you' of l. 12, and requires 'can'st.'

Or sprite, disdaine of such disdaine to haue!
Who for long faith, tho'² daily helpe I craue,
May get no almes, but scorne of beggerie.
V<u>ertue, awake! Beautie but beautie</u> is;
I may, I must, I can, I will, I do
Leaue following that which it is gaine to misse.
Let her goe!³ Soft, but here she comes! Goe to,
Vnkind, I loue you not! O me, that eye
Doth make my heart to giue⁴ my tongue the lie!

XLVIII.

'*Sweete cruell shot.*'

SOULE'S ioy, bend not those morning starres from
me,
W<u>here Vertue is made strong by Beautie's m</u>ight;
Where Loue is chastnesse, Paine doth learne⁵ delight,
And Humblenesse growes on with Majestie.   one

² In 2 qu. misprinted 'the.'
³ A and A 1613 misread 'do,' probably from the previous 'do'
and 'to.' I adopt 2 qu. 'Here' in Q 1 and A and A 1613,
'there' in Q 2—the latter a repetition of the 't' of 'but.'
⁴ So Q 1 and A 1613: 'give to,' Q 2, A and A 1605: 'former
preferable. 'The lie': 2 qu. badly 'a lie.'
⁵ Q 1, has the variant 'scorning youthes.'

Whateuer may ensue, O let me be
Copartner of the riches of that sight;
Let not mine eyes be hel-driv'n[6] from that light;
O looke, O shine, O let me die, and see.
For though I oft my selfe of them bemone
That through my heart their beamie darts be gone,
Whose curelesse wounds euen now most freshly bleed,
Yet since my death-wound is already got,
Deere killer, spare not thy sweete-cruell shot;
A kinde of grace it is to slaye with speed.

XLIX.

' I on my horse.'

I ON my horse, and Loue on me, doth[7] trie
    Our horsmanships, while by strange worke I proue
A horsman to my horse, a horse to Loue,
And now man's wrongs[8] in me, poor beast! descrie.
The raines wherewith my rider doth me tie

---

[6] Q 1 has 'blinded'—inferior.
[7] Agreeing with the nearer nominative, as in Latin.
[8] = the wrongs done by man I 'descrie' in me = myself.

Are humbled[9] thoughts, which bit of reuerence moue,
Curb'd-in with feare, but with guilt bosse aboue   gilt
Of hope, which makes it seeme faire to the eye:
The wand is will; thou, Fancie, saddle art,
Girt fast by Memorie; and while I spurre
My horse, he spurres with sharpe desire my hart;
He sits me fast, howeuer I do sturre;
And now hath made me to his hand so right,
That in the manage my selfe take delight.   menage

L.
Fulnesse of thoughts.'

STELLA, the fulnesse of my thoughts of thee
  Cannot be staid within my panting breast,
But they do swell and struggle forth of me,
Till that in words thy figure be exprest:
And yet, as soone as they so formèd be,
According to my lord Loue's owne behest,
With sad eies I their weake proportion see
To portrait that which in[1] this world is best.

---

[9] Better than 'reverent' of 2 qu.
[1] A and A 1613: 'what within,' 2 qu. indifferent, but text perhaps stronger.

So that I cannot chuse but write my mind,
And cannot chuse but put out what I write,
While these[2] poore babes their death in birth do find;
And now my pen these lines had dashèd quite,
But that they stopt his furie from the same,
Because their fore-front bare[3] sweet Stella's name.

LI.

' Pardon mine eares.'

PARDON mine eares, both I and they do pray,
    So may your tongue still flauntingly[4] proceed,
To them that do such entertainment need;
So may you still haue somewhat new to say.
On silly me do not the[5] burthen lay
Of all the graue conceits your braine doth breed;
But find some Hercules to beare, insteed

---

[2] qu. 'those'=sonnets of ll. 9-10: hence 'these,' as in A and A 1613.

[3] '*stopt* . . . . . *bare*'; 2 qu. 'stop . . . . . beares'; but 'had dashed' requires the former.

[4] 2 qu. 'fluently,' A and A 1613—the preferable, as it introduces something different from the 'new' of l. 4.

[5] 2 qu. 'your' wrongly.

Of Atlas tyrd, your wisedom's heav'nly sway.
For me,—while you discourse of courtly tides,
Of cunningst[6] fishers in most troubled streames,
Of straying waies,[7] when valiant Errour guides,—
Meanewhile my heart confers with Stella's beames,
And is e'en woe[8] that so sweet comedie
By such vnsuted speech should hindred be.

LII.

Vertue and Loue.

A STRIFE is growne between Vertue and Loue,
While each pretends that Stella must be his :
Her eyes, her lips, her all, saith Loue,[9] do this,
Since they do weare his badge, most firmely proue.
But Vertue thus that title doth disproue,
That Stella,—O deare name ! that Stella is

---

[6] 2 qu. a better reading decidedly than 'cunning,' and later than A and A 1613.

[7] 2 qu. misread 'waues'—a scribe's improvement, to be in (supposed) harmony with Fishers, &c.

[8] 2 qu. A and A 1613, inferiorly 'euen irkt.'

[9] 2 qu. 'Loue saith that he owes'=owns, but A and A 1613 preferable.

That vertuous soule, sure heire of heav'nly blisse,
Not this faire outside, which our heart doth moue :
And therefore, though her beautie and her grace
Be Loue's indeed, in Stella's selfe he may
By no pretence claime any manner place.[1]
Well, Loue, since this demurre our sute doth stay,
Let Vertue haue that Stella's selfe ; yet thus,
That Vertue but that body graunt to vs.

LIII.

'*What now, Sir Foole !*'

IN martiall sports I had my cunning tride,
 And yet to breake more staues did mee adresse,
While, with the people's shouts,[2] I must confesse,

---

[1] An archaism very common in Batman on Bartholomew: 'There is a manner running water' (l. 13, c. 21): 'And they [fishes] haue a manner lykenesse and kind [nature] of creeping, (c. 29) : 'And of adders is many manner kind ; and how many kind, so many manner venim ; and how many speces [species] so many manner malice, and so manner sores and aches, as there are colours, as Isid saith' (l. 18, c. 9).

[2] Q 1 has 'people shoutes,' and Q 2, 'while that the peopl's shoutes'—both erroneous. A and A 1613 adopted. This and the whole Sonnet suggested perhaps by Tasso, G. L. c. vi. st. 26-28.

Youth, lucke, and praise euen fil'd my veines with pride;
When Cupid, hauing me, his slaue, descride
In Marses liuery³ prauncing in the presse:
What now, Sir Foole! said he,—I would no lesse⁴:
Looke here, I say! I look'd, and Stella spide,
Who, hard by, made⁵ a window send forth light.
My heart then quak'd, then dazled were mine eyes,
One hand forgat to rule, th' other to fight,
Nor trumpet's sound I heard, nor friendly cries:
My foe came on, and beate the aire⁶ for me,
Till that her blush taught me my shame to see.

³ So in Sonnet xvii. The 2 qu. 'Mars his'—a transcriber's variant spelling. Sidney in Astrophel and Stella nowhere uses, if I err not, the falsely-supposed primitive form '—his.'

⁴ = I wanted nothing else than that epithet, I being filled with pride would have had it least of all things. The phrase is analogous to ''tis nothing less'= it is anything rather than (Richard II. act ii. sc. 2).

⁵ 2 qu. 'through.' The former preferable, because it does not so carry the mind to a candle behind a window, which is the light one generally sees 'through' a window, as to the sun's dazzling light that one so often sees (reflected but seemingly) in it. Stella, it must be remembered, is constantly ' his sun.'

⁶ = beat space instead of me in his prancing and feats of the manége. Shakespeare adapts and revises the phrase when Angelo

LIV.

'*They love indeed who quake to say they love.*'

BECAUSE I breathe not loue to euery one,
Nor doe not vse sette colours for to weare,
Nor nourish speciall locks of vowèd haire,[7]
Nor giue each speech a full point of a grone,
The Courtly nymphes, acquainted with the mone

(Measure for Measure, act ii. sc. 4) would rather be
'an idle plume
Which the air beats for vain.'
=which the air sways first one way and then another, as though it were an empty thing, lighter and more variable than itself. Both Sidney and Shakespeare doubtless thought of a Biblical phrase, 1 Corinthians, ix. 26.

[7] Here is explained the origin, apparently hitherto overlooked, of the after well-known 'love-locks,' though this at first love-Nazarite vow seems to have become a mere fashion. With, I presume, interruptions—for later writers seem to call it, or some variation of it, a newly-imported French custom—it lasted through several generations, preserved by the opposition it met with and by its having become a party badge. Every one will remember one 'Deformed,' who, as Dogberry says, they say 'wears a key in his ear and a lock hanging by it.' Here the 'key' was probably an earring, or it may have been a jewel attached to the 'lock'; for in early times at least the 'lock' was worn with a silk twist or ribbon in it, often probably the colour or gift of the lady-mistress.

Of them which in their lips Loue's standard beare :
What, he ! (say they of me) : now I dare sweare
He cannot loue ; no, no, let him alone.
And thinke so still, so Stella know my minde ;
Profess[8] in deede I do not Cupid's art ;
But you, fair maides, at length this true shall find,
That his right badge is but worne in the hart :
Dumbe swans, not chattring pies, do louers proue ;
They loue indeed who quake to say they love.

LV.

' Muses ... holy ayde.'

MUSES, I oft inuoked your holy[9] ayde,
With choisest flowers my speech to' engarland so,
That it, despisde,[1] in true but naked shew
Might winne some grace in your sweet grace[2] arraid ;
And oft whole troupes of saddest words I staid,

---

[8] 2 qu. 'protest.'
[9] Q 1, misprints 'whole,' and reads 'have crau'd.'
[1] 2 qu. badly 'disguisde.'
[2] For this second 'grace,' 2 qu. read 'skill ;' but as 'grace' is such a sought mannerism of the time, and agrees so much better with 'engarland,' I believe it a later change, as in A and A 1613.

Striuing abroad a-foraging to go,
Vntill by your inspiring I might know
How their blacke banner might be best displaid.
But now I meane no more your helpe to try,
Nor other sugring[3] of my speech to proue,
But on her name incessantly to cry ;
For let me but name her whom I doe loue,
So sweet sounds straight mine eare and heart do hit,
That I well finde no eloquence like it.

LVI.

'*Patience.*'

FY, schoole of Patience, fy! your lesson is
    Far, far too long to learne it without booke :
What, a whole weeke without one peece of looke,
And thinke I should not your large precepts misse !
When I might reade those letters faire of blisse
Which in her face teach vertue, I could brooke
Somwhat thy lead'n counsels, which I tooke
As of a friend that meant not much amisse.
But now that I, alas, doe want her sight,

---

[3] Cf. Son. xxv. l. 2 ; lix. l. 11 ; lxxiii. l. 5.

What, dost thou thinke that I can euer take
In thy cold stuffe⁴ a flegmatike delight?
No, Patience; if thou wilt my good, then make
Her come and heare with patience my desire,
And then with patience bid me beare my fire.

LVII.

' *My paines me reioyce.*'

WO hauing made, with many fights,⁵ his owne
   Each sence of mine, each gift, each power of mind;
Growne⁶ now his slaues, he forst them out to find
The thorowest words fit for Woe's selfe to grone,
Hoping that when they might finde Stella 'alone,⁷
Before she could prepare to be vnkind,
Her soule, arm'd but⁸ with such a dainty rind,

---

⁴ Q 1, badly misprints ' strife.'
⁵ Q 2, 'sighs.' The latter looks a tempting reading, but it is an error probably caused by influence of 'woe.' The context, especially l. 3, favours 'fights,' and Woe fighting by means of sighs is an image incongruous with that of slaves finding words fit for Woe's self to groan (l. 4).
⁶ =[being] growne.   ⁷ Cf. note on Son. xliv. l. 5.
⁸ Wrongly omitted in Q 1.

Should soone be pierc'd⁹ with sharpnesse of the mone.
She heard my plaints, and did not onely heare,
But them, so sweet is she, most sweetly sing,
With that faire breast making Woe's darknesse cleare..
A pretie case ; I hopèd her to bring
To feele my griefe ; and she, with face and voyce,
So sweets my paines, that my paines me reioyce.

LVIII.
Soueraignty.

DOUBT there hath beene when with his golden chaine
The orator so farre men's hearts doth bind,
That no pace else their guidèd steps can find
But as he¹ them more short or slack doth raine ;
Whether with words this souraignty he gaine,
Cloth'd with fine tropes, with² strongest reasons lin'd,

---

⁹ Better than ' hurt' (2 qu.), because, as evidenced by 'thorowest' and 'sharpnesse,' the words were to pierce like a lance or to winged arrows (ἔπεα πτερόεντα). See l. 9 of next Sonnet.

¹ 2 qu. 'in.' One cannot rein horses 'in' slack, and if one could, Sidney would have written 'them in.' Moreover with 'in' the expression is bad and obscure.

² 2 qu. 'as his'—a blunder from 'this' above.

Or else pronouncing grace,[3] wherewith his mind
Prints his owne liuely forme in rudest braine.
Now iudge by this : in piercing phrases late
Th' anatomy of all my woes I wrate ;
Stella's sweet breath the same to me did reed.
O voyce, O face ! maugre my speeche's might,
Which wooèd wo, most rauishing delight
Euen those sad words euen in sad me did breed.[4]

---

[3] *i.e.* [with] pronouncing grace. It may, however, be doubted whether Sidney intended the 'with' of ' with words' to be understood here, or whether it is to be taken out of 'wherewith.' This latter, though strange to us, can be exemplified by passages in our elder writers, who disliked such reduplications. See our DONNE; and there are these two from Henry Constable :

'An angell's face had angell's puritye,
And thou an angell's tongue didst speke withall.'
2d Sonnet to St. Katharyne.

'Yett, if those graces God to me impart
Which He inspyr'd thy blessèd brest withall.'
3d Sonnet to St. M. Magd.

where we should require [with] an angel's tongue, and [with] which—

[4] ll. 13-14. The construction is—Maugre the might of my sad speeches which wooed woe (ll. 5-6 and 9-10), even those sad words bred even in sad me ravishing delight when breathed by Stella's pronouncing grace (l. 7). The 2 qu. readings,

LIX.

'*More of a dog then me.*'

DEERE, why make you more of a dog then me?
If he doe loue, I burne,[5] I burne in loue;
If he waite well, I neuer thence would moue;
If he be faire, yet but a dog can be[6];
Little he is, so little worth is he;
He barks, my songs thine owne voyce oft doth proue;
Bidd'n, perhaps he fetchèd thee a gloue,
But I, vnbid, fetch euen my soule to thee.
Yet, while I languish, him that bosome clips,
That lap doth lap, nay lets, in spite of spite,
This sowre-breath'd mate taste of those sugred lips.
Alas, if you graunt onely such delight
To witlesse things, then Loue, I hope—since wit
Becomes a clog—will soone ease me of it.[7]

'With wooed words' most rauishing delight
Euen in bad mee a ioy to me did breede,'

do nothing with 'ravishing delight.' Hence 'with' is probably the frequent mistake for 'which,' due to the wth and w[ch] of MSS. The rest is puzzling; perhaps the conjectural change of some one who saw the sense intended, but could not construe the passage.

 2 qu. 'alas.'   [6] Supply [he] can be but a dog.
 [7] ll. 13-14: alluding, as does Donne, to the saying that a lover cannot be wise.

LX.

' Blest in my curse.'

WHEN my good angell guides me to the place
Where⁸ all my good I doe in Stella see,
That heau'n of ioyes throwes onely downe on me
Thundring⁹ disdaines and lightnings of disgrace;
But when the ruggedst step of Fortune's race
Makes me fall from her sight, then sweetly she,
With words wherein the Muses' treasures be,
Shewes loue and pitie to my absent case.
Now I, wit-beaten long by hardest fate,
So dull am, that I cannot looke into
The ground of this fierce loue and lovely¹ hate.
Then, some good body, tell me how I² do,
Whose presence absence, absence presence is;
Blest in my curse, and cursèd in my blisse.

---

⁸ Q 1, 'where's': Q 2, 'where': a mistake, the 's' of Q 1 was struck out and the faithful printer kept the (').

⁹ 2 qu. : and A 1613 seems to me to give, without intent, an unpleasant reference to her voice, whereas the allusion is to the black and thunder-bearing clouds of her disdainful looks. 'Lightnings' in plural rather than singular of 2 qu. agrees best with sense and with 'disdains' and 'glances.'

¹ 2 qu. misprint 'louing.'   ² 'I' is preferable to 'to' of 2 qu.

VOL. I.   F

LXI.

'Angel's sophistrie.'

OFT with true sighes, oft with vncallèd[3] teares,
    Now with slow words, now with dumbe eloquence,
I Stella's eyes assaid,[4] inuade her eares ;
But this, at last, is her sweet-breath'd defence :
That who indeed in-felt[5] affection beares,
So captiues to his saint both soule and sence,
That, wholly hers, all selfenesse[6] he forbeares,
Then his desires he learnes, his liue's course thence.[7]
Now, since her chast mind hates this loue in me,[8]
With chastned mind I straight must shew that she

---

  [3] =called forth on slight and insufficient provocation.

  [4] Same sense as 'assaild' of 2 qu.; but shows (what he supposed was the fact) less power in the attacking and less result on the attacked party.

  [5] Really felt in the soul, in the better self, not seated merely in the liver and flesh. This, therefore, is a better reading than 'sound,' 2 qu.

  [6] Query—a coinage by Sidney?

  [7] His desires are already existent, and she says 'then' he learns how evil those are, and 'then' learns what they should be. There is also a greater fulness of thought in 'then' and 'thence' than in 'thence' only, 2 qu.

  [8] As yet in the progress of his sonnets and of his love she has

Shall quickly me from what she hates remoue.
O Doctor Cupid, thou for me reply ;
Driu'n else to graunt, by angel's sophistrie, through
That I loue not without I leaue to loue.

LXII.

' Watred was my wine.'

LATE tyr'd with wo, euen ready for to pine
With rage of loue, I cald my Loue vnkind ;
She in whose eyes loue, though⁹ vnfelt, doth shine,
Sweet said, that¹ I true loue in her should find.

confessed no 'love' (2 qu.), but is a 'saint.' Cf. Sonnets lxii. lxvi.lxvii.lxix. Besides, she says, since her 'chaste mind' hates this love in Sidney, so he, if with in-felt affection he is captived to her with 'chast'ned mind,' then she can remove him from such love. And against 'this' (2 qu.) there are two arguments: (*a*) that there is no love of hers previously spoken of in the sonnet; (*b*) that the sentence is a continuation of her words repeated in the third person. In all these cases A and A 1613 give the better readings, and hence and from the same ' desires ' is preferable to 'desire' (2 qu.).

⁹ Q 1, ' loue's fyres '—inappropriate to her described state, and hence altered.

¹ This (A & A 1613) in rhythm is preferable to ' Sweetely said I,' especially as 'I' commences a new clause.

I ioyed; but straight thus watred was my wine:
That loue she did, but loued a loue² not blind;
Which would not let me, whom shee loued, decline
From nobler course, fit for my birth and mind:
And therefore, by her loue's authority,
Wild me these³ tempests of vaine loue to flie,
And anchor fast my selfe on Vertue's shore.
Alas, if this the only mettall be
Of loue new-coin'd to helpe my beggery,
Deere, loue me not, that you may loue me more.

LXIII.

'*No, no.*'

O GRAMMER-RULES, O now your vertues show;
So children still reade⁴ you with awfull eyes,
As my young doue may, in your precepts wise,

---

² This (A and A 1613) gives the sense intended, and such as is given by 2 qu.; but probably Sidney, who was fond of such repetitions, meant to alter 'with a loue' of 2 qu. to 'loued with loue,' and having left the words below, the editor struck out 'with' below 'loued,' instead of 'a.'

³ *i.e.* such as he mentions l. 2, and which caused her to speak; hence better than 'those' (2 qu.).

⁴ = So [may] children still read you.

ASTROPHEL AND STELLA. 85

Her graunt to me by her owne vertue[5] know :
For late, with heart most hie, with eyes most lowe,
I crau'd the thing which euer she denies ;
Shee, lightning loue, displaying Venus' skies,
Least once[6] should not be heard, twise said, No, no.
Sing then, my Muse, now Io Pæan[7] sing ;
Heau'ns enuy not at my high triumphing,
But grammer's force with sweete successe[8] confirme :
For grammer says,—O[9] this, deare Stella, say,—
For grammer sayes,—to grammer who sayes nay ?—
That in one speech two negatiues affirme !

LXIV.

' Do not will me from my loue to flie.'

NO more, my deare, no more these counsels trie ;
O giue my passions leaue to run their race ;
Let Fortune lay on me her worst disgrace ;

---

[5] =the grant which she has made to me by the vehemence of her vertue, which could not be contented without paying 'no' twice over.
[6] Contrasts better with 'twise' than 'one' of 2 qu.
[7] So Q 1 and A and A 1613 : 'I do' Q 2.
[8] =result, as frequently in those days.
[9] 2 qu. 'ah '—not Sidneian.

Let folke orecharg'd with braine against me crie;
Let clouds bedimme my face, breake in mine eye;
Let me no steps but of lost labour trace;[1]
Let all the earth with scorne recount my case,—
But do not will me from my loue to flie.
I do not enuie Aristotle's wit,
Nor do aspire to Cæsar's bleeding fame;
Nor ought do care though some aboue me sit;
Nor hope nor wish another course to frame,
But that which once may win thy cruell hart:
Thou art my wit, and thou my vertue art.

LXV.

'*Loue . . . vnkind.*'

LOUE, by sure proofe I may call the vnkind,
    That giu'st[2] no better ear to my iust cries;

---

[1] 2 qu. 'try'—the latter an error caught from the rhyme 'eye' above. So too in l. 7 'rase' is an error in 2 qu. for 'case,' for 'race' has already occurred in l. 2. Hence too I accept 'with' for 'in' in l. 7; but in l. 12 'with' of A and A 1613 is a misprint for 'wish' of 2 qu. In l. 5, Q 1 reads badly 'bereaues mine eyes.'

[2] 2 qu. 'That giues.' Old writers were not very accurate in this; but we adopt A and A 1613, especially as they are in other

Thou whom to me such my good turnes should bind,
As I may well recount, but none can prize :   price
For when, nak'd Boy, thou couldst no harbour finde
In this old world, growne now so too too³ wise,
I lodg'd thee in my heart, and being blind
By nature borne, I gaue to thee mine eyes ;
Mine eyes ! my light,⁴ my heart, my life, alas !
If so great seruices may scorned be,
Yet let this thought thy tygrish courage passe,⁵
That I perhaps am somewhat kinne to thee ;
Since in thine armes, if learnd fame truth hath⁶ spread,
Thou bear'st the arrow, I the arrow-head.⁷

points more correct, as l. 2, 'eare,' not 'eares' (which is not idiomatic English) : l. 3, ' should ' for 'shouldst' (2 qu.), where the transcriber has been misled by ' Thou,' the true nominative being ' good turns.'

³ Far more in manner of the day than ' to be ' (Q 2).

⁴ If one looks at ' eyes . . . . light,' it will be seen that ' heart . . . . life' (A and A 1613) is the better sequence, and more regular than 'life . . . . heart ' (2 qu.).

⁵ =over-pass, and therefore dominate.

⁶ Modern texts erroneously ' had.'

⁷ Cf. on Sonnet lxxii. l. 8.

LXVI.

' Hope to feede.'

AND do I see some cause a hope to feede,
    Or doth the tedious burd'n of long wo
In weakened minds quick apprehending breed[8]
Of euerie image which may comfort show?
I cannot brag of word, much lesse of deed,
Fortune wheeles[9] still with me in one sort slow;
My wealth no more, and no whit lesse my need;
Desier still on stilts of Feare doth go.

---

[8] The act of the faculty of apprehension seems better than 'apprehension' (2 qu.): and l. 12, 'looke' (2 qu.), is proved to be a mistake for 'look'd' by 'sent' (l. 11) and 'did' (l. 13), *e* having in several instances in these sonnets been read for *d*. But the rhythm of l. 8 leads me to adopt the reading of the 2 qu. with 'desier' as a trisyllable and 'the' omitted, and to think 'the' an editorial amendment.

[9] If we adopt 'Fortunes = Fortune's wheels,' 'slowe,' must be taken as a verb = go slow; but the 's' of wheels in Q 2 and A and A 1613, and in 'windes' of Q 1, leads me to imagine that 'Fortune wheels' (Q 2), where 'wheels' is a verb, is correct; for Fortune is only represented with one wheel. There is doubtless in this sonnet (ll. 6-7) a reminiscence of Sidney's loss of prospects by Leicester's; a loss which made him, in her friend's eyes, no longer a fit match for Stella; but it is here applied, as shown by the context, metaphorically, to his having received as yet nothing from her whence he could say he was enriched with her love.

And yet amid all feares a[1] hope there is,
Stolne to my hart since last faire night, nay day,
Stella's eyes sent to me the beames of blisse,
Looking on me while I lookt other way :
But when mine eyes backe to their heau'n did moue,
They fled with blush which guiltie seem'd of loue.

LXVII.

'*More truth, more paine.*'

HOPE, art thou true, or doest thou flatter me?
Doth Stella now beginne with pitious eye
The ruines of her conquest to espie?[2]
Will she take time before all wrackèd be?
Her eyes-speech[3] is translated thus by thee,

---

[1] Modern editions 'as '—an error.

[2] Stella had known well for days and months that she reigned over Sidney, her conquest; and 'pitious' (l. 2) and 'take time' (on which see onward), and 'wrackèd' (l. 4), all show the thought to be, Will she relent before her conquest be an utter ruin and waste? The 'this' (2 qu.) seems an error, for 'The ruins of this' &c. is bad rhythm, nor is there any antecedent to 'this.' It was probably a conjectural insertion and an attempt to amend the MS. here 'the raigne of her.'

[3] So 2 qu.=eye-speech: eyes' speech (A and A 1613 'eyes-speech') indifferent—for forms analogous to both are to be found.

But failst thou not in phrase so heau'nly hye?
Looke on againe, the faire[4] text better prie;
What blushing notes dost thou in margine see?
What sighes stolne out, or kild before full-borne?
Hast thou found such and such-like arguments,
Or art thou else to comfort me forsworne?
Well, how-so thou interpret the contents,
I am resolu'd thy errour to maintaine,
Rather then by more truth to get more paine.

LXVIII.

'Planet of my light.'

STELLA, the onely planet of my light,
    Light of my life, and life of my desire,
Chiefe good whereto my hope doth only 'aspire,
World of my wealth, and heau'n of my delight;
Why dost thou spend the treasures[5] of thy sprite
With voice more fit to wed Amphion's lyre,
Seeking to quench in me the noble fire
Fed by thy worth,[6] and kindled by thy sight?

---

[4] 2 qu. 'fine,' which is better than 'true' (A and A 1613).
[5] Better than 'treasure' (2 qu.).
[6] 2 qu. 'Set . . . wrath.' The latter mere errors. He has

And all in vaine : for while thy breath most sweet
With choisest words, thy words with reasons rare,
Thy reasons firmly set on Vertue's feet,
Labour to kill in me this killing care :
O thinke I then, what paradise of ioy
It is, so faire a vertue to enjoy !

LXIX.

Coucnant.

O IOY too high for my low stile[7] to show !
O blisse fit for a nobler state[8] then me !

called her 'wrath' still lovely, but throughout it is her 'worth' as well as beauty that makes him love; her beauty inflames, and her worth keeps up the flame. 'Kindled' (2 qu.) corrects a very noticeable error of A and A 1613 of 'blinded.' But Q 1 makes a worse mistake in l. 14, by reading 'annoy' for 'enioy'; also in l. 11 the 2 qu. badly misprint 'are' for 'on.' In l. 6 we have ˇAmphiŏn : in 3d Song, l. 4, ˉAmphiŏn—noted as a caution to those who find so many proofs of Shakespeare's lack of learning in such things.

[7] 2 qu. misprint 'loue still.' His loue has not 'still' or continually shown joy, but only 'woe.' This sonnet marks his first certainty of being loved (cf. Sonnet lxx. l. 2). The word 'high' shows the antithetical 'low style' to be the true reading. He has several times spoken of his 'stile' as uninfluenced by the beauties with which others adorn their songs: and cf. next line also.

[8] This constantly so-used Elizabethan word is better than 'seat' of 2 qu.

Enuie, put out thine eyes, least thou do see
What oceans of delight in me do[9] flowe !
My friend, that oft saw through all maskes my wo,
Come, come, and let me powre my selfe on thee.
Gone is the Winter of my miserie !
My Spring appeares ; O see what here doth grow :
For Stella hath, with words where faith doth shine,
Of her high heart giu'n me the monarchie :
I, I, O I, may say that she is mine !
And though she giue but thus conditionly,
This realme of blisse while vertuous[1] course I take,
No kings be crown'd but they some couenants make.

LXX.

' Wise silence.'

M Y Muse may well grudge at my heau'nly ioy,
    Yf still I force her in sad rimes to creepe :
She oft hath drunk my teares, now hopes to enioy
Nectar of mirth, since I Ioue's[2] cup do keepe.

---

[9] 2 qu. ' doth '—usual error through influence of delight.

[1] Better than ' vertue's ' (2 qu.)—each of which would produce the other, because it is ' virtuous ' course in especial reference to this love.   [2] Modern editions ' Loue's '—without authority.

Sonets be not bound prentise to annoy;
Trebles sing high, so well as bases deepe;
Griefe but Loue's winter-liuerie is; the boy
Hath cheekes to smile, so well as eyes to weepe.[3]
Come then, my Muse, shew thou[4] height of delight
In well-raisde notes; my pen, the best it may,
Shall paint out ioy, though but in blacke and white.
Cease, eager Muse; peace, pen, for my sake stay,
I giue you here my hand for truth of this,—
Wise silence is best musicke vnto blisse.

LXXI.

Inward sunne.

WHO will in fairest booke of Nature know
How vertue may best lodg'd in beautie be,
Let him but learne of Loue to reade in thee,
Stella, those faire lines which true goodnesse show.

[3] Lines 6 and 8, 'so' 2 qu.: 'as,' A and A 1613: former more archaic.

[4] Sidney never could write 'shew the height of delight' (2 qu.). The corrector probably altered 'force' (Q 1) to 'height,' but omitted to change 'the' (Q 1) to 'thou.'

There shall he find all vices'⁵ ouerthrow,
Not by rude force, but sweetest soueraigntie
Of reason, from whose light those night-birds flie,
That inward sunne in thine eyes shineth so.
And, not content to be Perfection's heire
Thy selfe, doest striue all minds that way to moue,
Who marke in thee what is in thee⁶ most faire :
So while thy beautie drawes⁷ the heart to loue,
As fast thy vertue bends that loue to good :
But, ah, Desire still cries, Giue me some food.

⁵ As shown by 'night-birds, and vices,' the better reading is 'those' not 'these' (2 qu.) ; for night-birds and owls, or the like, do not fly Stella, but those owl-vices do.

⁶ A and A 1613—the usual mannerism repetition, and though Q 2 may be a variant ('in deede'), it is open to the suspicion that part only of Q 1 was corrected. It is also in favour of 'in thee' being a later change, that all the readings of A and A 1613 in this sonnet are better than those of 2 qu.

⁷ A and A 1613, agrees better with 'bends' than 'driues' (2 qu.). And 'the heart'=the hearts of all minds which all strive, the word being used generally, better than 'my.' He does not now speak of his heart only : his particular addition comes in l. 14.

LXXII.

'My onely Deare.'

DESIRE, though thou my old companion art,
And oft so clings to my pure loue that I
One from the other scarcely can discrie,
While[8] each doth blowe the fier of my hart ;
Now from thy fellowship I needs must part ;
Venus is taught with Dian's wings to flie ;
I must no more in thy sweet passions lie ;
Vertue's gold now must head my Cupid's dart.[9]
Seruice and honour, wonder with delight,
Feare to offend, will[1] worthie to appeare,
Care shining in mine eyes, faith in my sprite ;
These things are left me by my onely Deare :
But thou, Desire, because thou wouldst haue all,
Now banish art ; but yet, alas, how shall ?[2]

---

[8] = And both of you blowe.

[9] A reference to the arms assigned by fanciful heralds to Cupid, the Love spoken of.

[1] 2 qu. and modern editions 'well'; but this makes nonsense. The true reading (A and A 1613) is undoubtedly 'will': (*a*) because 'will,' generally used in a bad sense = sensual will (as in Shakespeare's Sonnets), is here spoken of as a purified will worthy to appear : (*b*) because each of the three lines, ll. 9-11, is made up of two clauses.

[2] Either for shalt, metri gr., or = how shall I banish thee ?

LXXIII.

' Kisse.'

L OUE, still a Boy, and oft a wanton is,
    School'd onely by his mother's tender eye ;
What wonder then if he his lesson misse,
When for so soft a rodde deare play he trye ?
And yet my Starre, because a sugred kisse   Stella
In sport I suckt[3] while she asleepe did lye,
Doth lowre, nay chide, nay threat for only this.
Sweet, it was saucie Loue, not humble I.[4]
But no 'scuse serues ; she makes her wrath appeare
In Beautie's throne : see now, who dares come neare
Those scarlet Iudges, threatning bloudie paine.
O heau'nly foole,[5] thy most kisse-worthy face
Anger invests with such a louely grace,
That Anger's selfe[6] I needs must kisse againe.

---

[3] 2 qu. misread ' sucke.'

[4] Q 1 has 'that pest so nye'—an early variant, but not so good as A and A 1613, because it does not clearly disjoin Love from Sidney's self.

[5] ' *O heau'nly fool* ' and cf. Shakespeare " And my poor fool" &c.

[6] A 1613 ' Anger selfe.'

LXXIV.

'*I am no pickpurse of another's wit.*'

I NEUER dranke of Aganippe well,
Nor euer[7] did in shade of Tempe sit,
And Muses scorne with vulgar brains to dwell;
Poore layman I, for sacred rites vnfit.
Some doe I heare of poets' furie tell,
But, God wot, wot not what they meane by it;
And this I sweare by blackest brooke[8] of hell,
I am no pick-purse of another's wit.
How falles it then, that with so smooth an ease
My thoughts I speake; and what I speake doth flow
In verse, and that my verse best wits doth please?
Ghesse we the cause? What, is it this? Fie, no.
Or so? Much lesse. How then? Sure thus it is,
My lips are sweet,[9] inspired with Stella's kisse.

---

[7] This recurrence from Q 2 to Q 1 and Sonnet lxiii. make me discard 'neuer' (Q 2) as a transcriber's variant. [8] = Styx:
'Umbrarum hic locus est, Somni Noctisque soporæ.' *Æn*. vi. 390.
and he swears by it the strictest oath of the gods:
  'Dii cujus jurare timent et fallere numen.' *Ib*. 324.
[9] 2 qu. 'sure.' The latter jars so much with 'sure' (l. 13), that I regard it as a memory error: the pause too after 'sweet' gives a better closing rhythm.

LXXV.

' Edward IV.'

OF all the kings that euer here did raigne,
    Edward, named fourth, as first in praise, I name :
Not for his faire outside, nor well-lined braine,
Although lesse gifts impe feathers oft on fame. *join, add on*
Nor that he could, young-wise, wise-valiant, frame
His sire's reuenge, ioyn'd with a kingdome's gaine ;
And gain'd by Mars, could yet mad[10] Mars so tame,
That balance weigh'd, what sword did late obtaine.
Nor that he made the floure-de-luce so 'fraid,
—Though strongly hedg'd—of bloudy lyons' pawes,
That wittie Lewes to him a tribute paid :   *wise*
Nor this, nor that, nor any such small cause ;
But only for this worthy knight[1] durst proue
To lose his crowne, rather then faile his loue.

---

[10] Q 1 'make.'

[1] 2 qu. 'king.' He has already called him 'king,' and now speaks not of his kingly acts, but of his chivalrous devotion as a true 'knight.' Line 6 refers to his reconquest of the crown ; l. 8 to his attempts to reform abuses in the law-courts, so that justice might weigh with equal scales : l. 11 to his after-war with France, though the hedging of the fleur-de-lys with lions' paws is somewhat of an anachronism if it refer to the Lancastrian English, for

LXXVI.

'Gentle force.'

SHE comes, and streight therewith her shining twins do moue
Their rayes to me, who in their tedious absence lay
Benighted[2] in cold wo ; but now appears my day,
The onely light of ioy, the only warmth of loue.
She comes with light and warmth, which, like Aurora, proue
Of gentle force,[3] so that mine eyes dare gladly play
With such a rosie morne, whose beames, most freshly gay,
Scorch not, but onely doe dark chilling sprites remoue.

they as a party had been broken some time previously; l. 14 refers to his marriage with Lady Elizabeth Grey, whence, as is well known, the defection of the King-maker took its rise.

[2] Q 1 has 'Bathde': Q 2 'benighted': 2 qu. 'shining.' With 'benighted' in 'shining' there is a foot too much. I apprehend Sidney's earlier words may have been 'Bathde . . . . shining'; but as they made Stella, his sun, too decidedly masculine and himself feminine, he altered as in text.

[3] Which in l. 5 refers to light and warmth. Therefore 'force,' A and A 1613, not 'face' (Q 1). We should say Aurora's. 'Mine' is better here than 'my' (2 qu).

But, lo, while I do speake, it groweth noone with me,
Her flamie-glistring[4] lights increase with time and place,
My heart cries, oh ![5] it burnes, mine eyes now dazled be
No wind, no shade can coole : what helpe then in my
   case ?
But with short breath, long looks, staid feet, and
   aching[6] hed,
Pray that my sunne goe downe with meeker[7] beames to
   bed.

[4] 2 qu. 'glittering.'
[5] 'Ah' A and A 1613 : 'oh' Q 2 : 'O' Q 1.
[6] '*aching*,' in A and A 1613 and Q 2 'walking': in Q 1 'waking.' I read (*meo periculo*) 'aching,' knowing how spread-out and difficult Sidney's handwriting was. Nothing is more common than headache from an over-fierce sun. It might be 'watching,' but *a*ching might easily be misread 'wa.' My friend Mr. Thomson of Edinburgh (as before) writes me here:—"'*Aching*' is a very plausible conjecture ; but the construction of the line is antithetical—*short* breath, *long* looks, *staid* feet, ... head. Some word implying motion is surely required, as the epithet to 'head,' and 'walking' is perhaps not indefensible. It was then apparently used to signify other motions than the locomotive kind to which it is now confined : *e. g.* 'her tongue did *walk*' (F. Q. B. II. c. iv. st. 5) ; so that it might very well express what we now call throbbing."
[7] '*meeker*' (Q 1), to which A and A 1613 return ; 'mee her' (Q 2) being stark naught, though an easy error. Sidney going to bed with her hot beams would have been a male Semele.

LXXVII.

' A meane price.'

THOSE lookes, whose beames be ioy, whose motion
    is delight ;
That face, whose lecture shews[8] what perfect beauty is ;
That presence, which doth giue darke hearts a liuing
    light ;
That grace, which Venus weeps that she her selfe doth
    misse ;
That hand, which without touch holds more then Atlas
    might ;   than
Those lips, which make death's pay a meane price for
    a kisse ;
That skin, whose passe-praise[9] hue scornes this poor
    tearm of white ;
Those words, which do sublime the quintessence of
    bliss ;
That voyce, which makes the soule plant himselfe in
    the eares ;
That conuersation sweet, where such high comforts be,

---

[8] Cf. Donne's 'Loue-Lecture' (Vol. ii. 440-1).
[9] A and A 1613 : 'past-praise,' Q 2 : 'passing,' Q. 1.

As, consterd in true speech, the name of heav'n it
  beares;
Makes me in my best thoughts and quietst[1] iudgments
  see
That in no more but these I might be fully blest :
Yet, ah, my mayd'n Muse doth blush to tell the best.

LXXVIII.[2]

'Ielousie.'

O HOW the pleasant ayres of true loue be
  Infected by those vapours which arise
From out that noysome gulfe, which gaping lies
Betweene the iawes of hellish Ielousie!
A monster, others' harme, selfe-miserie,

---

[1] '*quietst*,' A and A 1613 : stronger than 'quiet' (2 qu.), and better agreeing with 'best': 'judgments' (2 qu.) agrees with 'thoughts,' and both allow of the thought of what was the fact, that he now has best thoughts and quietest judgments, now worse thoughts and unquiet judgments, troubled by the influence of desire—that he is, in fact, swayed to and fro.

[2] Sonnet lxxviii. This sonnet is wretchedly given in both quartos, *e. g.* they misprint in l. 5 'harms' for 'harme': l. 7, 'heart' for ' hurt': l. 8, 'injuries' for 'injurie': l. 11, 'though still' for ' stirre still '—continually.

Beautie's plague, Vertue's scourge, succour of lies ;
Who his owne ioy to his owne hurt applies,
And onely cherish doth with injurie :
Who since he hath, by Nature's speciall grace,
So piercing pawes as spoyle when they embrace ;
So nimble feet as stirre still, though on thornes ;
So many eyes, ay seeking their owne woe ;
So ample eares as neuer good newes know : [3]
Is it not euill[4] that such a diuell wants hornes ?

LXXIX.

'Sweetnesse.'

SWEET kisse, thy sweets I faine would sweetly' endite,
Which, euen of sweetnesse sweetest sweetner[5] art ;

---

[3] A very curious double instance in Q 1 (partly uncorrected in Q 2) of taking a word from line below. Q 1 has, l. 12, 'as' for 'aye,' taking it from 'as' of l. 13, and for 'as' of l. 13 is taken 'that' from l. 14. Q 2 corrects l. 12 to 'aye,' but did not correct l. 13.

aye	as	aye
as	that	that
that	that	that
A and A 1613.	Q 1.	Q 2.

[4] '*euill*' : 2 qu. 'ill.' Sidney, like Southwell, used 'euill' as a monosyllable. [5] '*sweetner*' : 2 qu. 'sweeter'—the latter inferior. See also on next Sonnet, l. 6.

Pleasingst consort,[6] where each sence holds a part;
Which, coupling doues, guides Venus' chariot right.
Best charge, and brauest retrait in Cupid's fight;[7]
A double key, which opens[8] to the heart,
Most rich when most his riches it impart;
Nest of young ioyes, schoolmaster of delight,
Teaching the meane at once to take and giue;
The friendly fray, where blowes both[9] wound and heale,
The prettie death, while each in other liue.
Poore hope's first wealth, ostage[1] of promist weale;
Breakefast of loue. But lo, lo, where she is,
Cease we to praise; now pray we for a kisse.

[6] '*consort*' = a tune in parts. A consort of music cannot have anything to do with 'coupling doves,' and this shows our punctuation 'part'; is correct, and that l. 4 is a new clause and thought. 'Which,' therefore (not 'With,' Q 2) is the analogue of 'Which' l. 2, and the sense is 'Which being coupling doues,' or 'Which coupling doves together thus guides.' The allusion is to the representations of Venus's chariot drawn by billing doves.

[7] Q 2 'sight'—a printer's error.

[8] '*opens*': 'openeth,' 2 qu. Indifferent, but it seems to me that 'opens' is, so to speak, more transitive. A door 'openeth' or 'opens' to, a key opens to, *i.e.* opens the door to.

[9] 'do' Q 2. Text more expressive.

[1] = hostage = pledge; but 'ostage' is clearly the later revisal of 'pledge' (Q 1). Moreover 'pledge,' if taken in sense of 'oath,' is, and especially in Sidney's case was, too strong.

LXXX.

'*Sweet lipp.*'

SWEET-SWELLING lip, well maist thou swell in pride,[2]
Since best wits thinke it wit[3] thee to admire;
Nature's praise, Vertue's stall; Cupid's cold fire,
Whence words, not words but heav'nly graces slide;
The new Pernassus, where the Muses[4] bide;
Sweetner[5] of musicke, Wisedome's beautifier,

---

[2] Cf. Song 2, vi. i.
[3] 'best' (Q 1) probably original reading, but 'wit' (Q 2 and A and A 1613) later and better.
[4] 'graces' in Q 1, caught from line above.
[5] '*sweetner*': 'sweetness,' 2 qu. The latter an error. Her lips are not represented so much as the 'sweetness' of music in what they utter, but as 'sweetness' of what was already music, whether the music were *ab intra* or *ab extra*, and it agrees with the next -er forms, including 'fastner.' 'Fastness'=fortress would, in the language of that day, be a very equivocal compliment, as may be judged from the account of the tilt before Queen Elizabeth in 1581, when Sidney was a Knight of Desire. Besides a person, or part of a person, may be said to be dyed in grain, but a fortress so dyed is absurd; and that 'fastner' was the original word is shown because it suggested the remembrance of the 'mordants' used to fasten colours in dyeing, and so suggested the pretty thought of dyeing Beauty's blush in Honour's grain.

Breather of life, and fastner of desire,
Where Beautie's blush in Honor's graine[6] is dide.
Thus much my heart compeld my mouth to say;
But now, spite of my heart, my mouth[7] will stay,
Loathing all lies, doubting[8] this flatterie is:
And no spurre can his resty[9] race renewe,
Without,[1] how farre this praise is short of you,
Sweet lipp, you teach my mouth with one sweet kisse.

---

[6] See longer Notes and Illustrations (*c*) at close.

[7] '*mouth*': better than 'tongue' (2 qu.), because the line runs parallel with the previous one, and because the subject of the sonnet is not the 'tongue' as a speaker, but the 'lip,' and also because there is a reference to St. Matthew xii. 34.

[8] =suspecting: its frequent meaning at that time.

[9] '*his resty*,' *i.e.* his, the mouth's, race now resty: 'this,' 2 qu. —often miswritten for 'his'—rather includes the whole that race, ll. 1-8, where out of the abundance of the heart the mouth spoke —a race anything but 'resty.' 'Resty'=restive, staying or stopping, and therefore stubborn. It is so used in a translation of Calvin, and so Chapman, &c. (ll. b. 5): Richardson *s.v.* The variations of Q 1 are all early: l. 3, 'stall' is used, it must be remembered, for a cathedral or church stall, as well as for an oxstall. Query—any inner reference to the 'stable' and 'manger' of Bethlehem?

[1] Construction is, Without, sweet lip, you teach with a kiss, how far, &c.

LXXXI.
' Still, still, kiss.'

O KISSE, which dost those ruddie gemmes impart,
    Or gemmes[2] or fruits of new-found Paradise,
Breathing all blisse, and sweetning[3] to the heart,
    Teaching dumbe lips a nobler exercise ;—
O kisse, which soules, euen soules, together ties
    By linkes of loue and only Nature's art,
How faine would I paint thee to all men's eyes.
    Or of thy gifts at least shade out some part !
But she forbids ; with blushing words she sayes
    She builds her fame on higher-seated praise.
But my heart burnes ; I cannot silent be.
    Then, since, dear life, you faine would haue me peace,
And I, mad with delight, want wit to cease,
    Stop you my mouth with still, still kissing me.[4]

---

[2] Q 1 ' ioyes.'
[3] '*sweetning*': 'sweetness,' 2 qu. The meaning of this is evident, but 'sweetning' divides the thought, and makes two of it. The kiss breathes all bliss, and is also 'sweetning' to the heart. Hence 'sweetning' the later elaboration.
[4] In a note on the following lines of his Ivy Church :
'Eccho could not now to the last woord yeild any eccho,
  All opprest with loue, for her ould loue stil she remembred,
  And she remembred stil that sweete Narcissus her ould loue,'

LXXXII.

'Cherries.'

NYMPH of the gard'n where all beauties be,—
Beauties which do in excellencie passe
His who till death lookt⁵ in a watrie glasse,
Or hers whom nakd the Troian boy did see; Venus
Sweet-gard'n-nymph, which keepes the cherrie-tree
Whose fruit doth farre th' Esperian⁶ tast surpasse,
Most sweet-faire, most faire-sweete, do not, alas,
From comming neare those⁷ cherries banish mee.

Fraunce gets quaintly irate with those who had objected that 'stil' had been repeated for the sake of the metre, and tells them that one is an adverb and one an adjective, and to express his meaning and his sarcasm in one, he says, 'and they might as well be *stil* and not speake any thing, as *stil* talk and yet say nothing.' Perhaps Sidney, in saying 'she would have him be silent' (l. 12), intended the like conceit in 'still, still kissing'=be continually silent-kissing me—kissing, not with an ordinary kiss, but with the silent-pressing kiss of passionate love.

⁵ Error of Q 1, Q 2 is 'lock't.'   ⁶ =Hesperian.

⁷ '*those*': better than 'these' (2 qu.), because he wishes to approach those cherries from which he is kept. In a very unlikely place, viz. in Hausted's *Rivall Friends* (1632), we have a vivid 'cherry' metaphor worthy of note here for the student-reader.

For though, full of desire, empty of wit,—
Admitted late by your best-gracèd grace,
I caught at one of them, and⁸ hungry bit;
Pardon that fault; once more grant me the place;
And I do sweare, euen by the same delight,
I will but kisse; I neuer more will bite.

LXXXIII.

To a Sparrow.

GOOD brother Philip,⁹ I haue borne you long;
I was content you should in fauour creepe,

---

⁸ '*and*.' I have ventured on but one conjectural emendation thus far. Here the last line seems to demand that the 'an' of 2 qu. or 'a,' should be 'and.' Without this, the promise not to bite loses its force, and comes upon one unintelligibly. It is evident too that he calls her lips cherries to enable him to speak of the bite-kiss that he gave.

⁹ Line 1 and l. 14: A and A 1613 read 'Philip' as a dissyllable in l. 1, and 'Phip' a monosyllable in l. 14. The 2 qu. reverse this, and hence the other changes, 'forborne,' l. 1, and the omission of 'off,' l. 14. Philip in full seems more correct with brother, and Sir Phip when he addresses him finely as a sparrow and sharply—Phillip, Phip.

'*Gurney.* Good leave, good Philip.
Bastard.   Phillip !—sparrow !—James,
There's toys abroad.'   King John, act i. sc. 1.

While craftely you seem'd your cut[1] to keepe,
As though that faire soft hand did you great wrong:
I bare with enuie, yet I bare[2] your song,
When in her necke you did loue-ditties peepe;
Nay—more foole I—oft suffered you to sleepe
In lillies' neast where Loue's selfe lies along.
What, doth high place ambitious thoughts augment?
Is sawcinesse reward of curtesie?
Cannot such grace your silly selfe content,
But you must needs with those lips billing be,
And through those lips drinke nectar from that toong?
Leaue that, Syr Phip, least off your neck be wroong!

He being now Sir Richard. See also Skelton's Phyllyp sparowe, and Lyly's Mother Bombie, a sparrow being so called on account of his 'peep, peep' (l. 6), when, as Catullus says, pipilabit.

[1] See longer Notes and Illustrations (*d*) at close.

[2] Looking to 'bare' and 'borne' (l. 1) 'beare' is a careless error for 'bare' (2 qu.).

LXXXIV.

'My Muse.'

HIGH way, since you my chiefe Pernassus³ be,
And that my Muse, to some eares not vnsweet,⁴
Tempers her words to trampling horses' feete
More oft⁵ then to a chamber-melodie.
Now, blessèd you beare onward blessèd me
To her, where I my heart, safe-left,⁶ shall meet ;
My Muse and I must you of dutie greet
With thankes and wishes, wishing thankfully.
Be you still faire, honourd by publicke heede ;⁷

---

³ '*Pernassus.*' So in the 'Return from Pernassus,' 1606, Ascham in Toxophilus, &c.

⁴ '*vnsweet*': 2 qu. 'unmeet.' As he is speaking of his Muse, and as we have the rhyme 'meet' (l. 6), I think 'vnsweet' the right word (A and A 1613), or at all events the later and better one.

⁵ '*oft*': 'often,' 2 qu.—a syllable too much. Sidney rarely, if ever, elides the -en, except in 'heaven' and 'even,' which are constantly, if not always, monosyllabic.

⁶ '*safe-left*' (A and A 1613) is prettier than 'safe-best' (2 qu.) = with Stella.

⁷ From the better rhythm and the other changes, 'faire, honour'd' (A and A 1613) is later, but I am not sure that 'carefull kept' (2 qu.) does not give a better sense.

By no encrochment wrong'd, nor time forgot ;
Nor blam'd for bloud, nor sham'd for sinfull deed ;
And that you know I enuy you no lot
Of highest wish, I wish you so much bliss,—
Hundreds of yeares you Stella's feet may kisse.

LXXXV.
'*Kingly tribute.*'

I SEE the house,—my heart thy selfe containe ![8]
    Beware full sailes drowne not thy tottring barge,
Least ioy, by nature apt sprites to enlarge,
Thee to thy wracke beyond thy limits straine ;
Nor do like lords whose weake confusèd braine,
Not 'pointing to fit folkes each vndercharge,   appointing
While euerie office themselues will discharge,
With doing all, leaue nothing done but paine.
But giue apt seruants their due place : let eyes
See beautie's totall summe summ'd in her[9] face ;

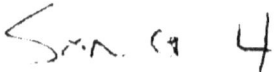

---

[8] Lines 1, 4-5 and 7, Q 1 gives these early readings : 'Behold my heart the house that thee contains' : 'shames' : 'braines' : 'Striue in themselues each office to.'

[9] 2 qu.—misprint 'their.'

[1]Let eares heare speach which wit to wonder ties ;[2]
Let breath sucke vp those sweetes; let armes embrace
The globe of weale, lips Lou's indentures make;
Thou but of all the kingly tribute take.

LXXXVI.

'Sweet ludge.'

ALAS, whence came[3] this change of lookes? If I
Haue chang'd desert, let mine owne conscience be
A still-felt plague to selfe-condemning mee;
Let woe gripe on my heart, shame loade mine eye :
But if all faith, like spotlesse ermine, ly
Safe in my soule, which only doth to thee,

---

[1] ' Let eares hear that speech which ties wit to wonder '—unites wisdom or knowledge to wonder, while ' unites will ' (2 qu.) is meaningless.

[2] Lines 9-11, ' *eyes* . . . . . *ties*.' This recurrence of A and A 1613 to Q 1 alone proves 'eye . . . tie' (Q 2) to be wrong ; but there are other two proofs : ' Eares, arms, and lips ' are all in the plural, and ' speech' which requires ' ties.' The change is one of those quasi-grammatical alterations by a transcriber, founded here on the mistake that ' eares ' is the nominative to ' ties.'

[3] 2 qu. ' comes '—indifferent.

As his sole obiect of felicitie,
With wings of loue in aire of wonder flie,
O ease your hand, treate not so hard your slave;
In iustice paines come not till faults do call:
Or if I needs, sweet Iudge, must torments haue,
Vse something else to chast'n me withall
Then those blest eyes, where all my hopes do dwell:
No doome should[4] make one's[5] heau'n become his hell.

LXXXVII.[6]

' Duetie to depart.'

WHEN I was forst from Stella euer deere— [heart
  Stella, food of my thoughts, hart of my hart—
Stella, whose eyes make all my tempests[7] cleere—
By Stella's lawes of duetie to depart;
Alas, I found that she with me did smart;
I saw that teares did in her eyes appeare;
I sawe that sighes her sweetest lips did part,

[4] 2 qu. 'shall'—wrong.
[5] 2 qu.—better than 'once' (A and A 1613), albeit 'one' is defensible. [6] See longer Notes and Illustrations (e) at close.
[7] 2 qu. perversely misprint 'temples.'

And her sad words my sadded[8] sense did heare.
For me, I wept[9] to see pearles scattered so ;
I sigh'd her sighes, and wailèd for her wo ;
Yet swam in ioy, such loue in her was seene.
Thus, while th' effect most bitter was to me,
And nothing then the cause more sweet could be,
I had bene vext, if vext I had not beene.

LXXXVIII.[1]

'Absence.'

OUT, traytor Absence, darest thou counsell me
From my deare captainesse to run away,
Because in braue array heere marcheth she,
That, to win mee, oft shewes a present pay ?
Is faith so weake ? or is such force in thee ?
When sun is hid, can starres such beames display ?
Cannot heav'n's food, once felt, keepe stomakes free
From base desire on earthly cates to pray ?   prey
Tush, Absence ; while thy mistes eclipse that light,
My orphan sense flies to the inward sight,

---

[8] More vivid than 'saddest' (A and A 1613).
[9] a qu. ' weep '—the frequent error of *d* or *t* final being omitted.
[1] See longer Notes and Illustrations (*f*) at close.

Where memory sets foorth the beames of loue;
That, where before hart loued and eyes did see,
In hart both sight and loue now couplèd be:
Vnited powers make each the stronger proue.

LXXXIX.

'*Day and Night.*'

NOW that of absence the most irksom night
  With darkest shade doth ouercome my day[2];
Since Stella's eyes, wont[3] to giue me my day,
Leauing my hemisphere, leaue[4] me in night;
Each day seemes long, and longs for long-staid night;
The night, as tedious, wooes th' approch of day:
Tired[5] with the dusty toiles of busie day,
Languisht with horrors of the silent night;
Suffering the euils both of day and night,
While no night is more darke then is my day,

---

  [2] '*my day*': as he is speaking metaphorically, and of his own day or state, 'my day' is much preferable to 'the' (2 qu.).

  [3] Q 1 inadvertently inserts 'that' before 'wont'—non-metrical.

  [4] Q 1 reads 'o'recast with': Q 2 'reaues me': 'eyes' of l. 3 demands 'leaue,' not 'leaues.'   [5] '*toyled*' for 'tird.'

Nor no day hath lesse quiet then my night:
With such bad-mixture of my night and day,
That liuing thus in blackest Winter night,
I feele the flames⁶ of hottest Sommer day.

XC.

'Fame.'

STELLA, thinke not that I by verse seeke fame,
   Who seeke, who hope, who loue, who liue but
      thee⁷;
Thine eyes my pride, thy lips mine history:
If thou praise not, all other praise is shame.

⁶ Q 1 'gleames'—all these earlier. In ll. 7-14 Sidney at the close of this sentence seems to have forgotten how he began to construct it. At least I cannot construe it satisfactorily to myself.

⁷ '*liue but thee*': this is strange, but not stranger than 'hope but thee,' and as prepositions 'to,' 'for,' &c. were often omitted in Elizabethan English, so is it more allowable here to omit 'for' or 'in' where the other conjoined verbs do not require either. 'Like' (2 qu.) is an anti-climax and worse after 'loue.' In l. 9 'Ne' (A and A 1613) agrees better than 'Nor' of 2 qu. with the somewhat archaic sentence in which it is placed: but 'could I' (2 qu.) is better than 'I could' of A and A 1613: and so, l. 10, the transposition of 2 qu. better than 'to me thereof.'

Nor so ambitious am I, as to frame
A nest for my young praise in lawrell tree :
In truth, I sweare I wish not there should be
Graued in my epitaph a Poet's name.
Ne, if I would, could I iust title make,
That any laud thereof to me should growe,
Without my plumes from others' wings I take :
For nothing from my wit or will doth flow,
Since all my words thy beauty doth endite,
And Loue doth hold my hand, and makes me write.

XCI.

'You in them I love.'

STELLA, while now, by Honour's cruell might,
    I am from you, light of my life,[8] misled,
And whiles,[9]—faire you, my sunne, thus ouerspred
With Absence' vaile,—I liue in Sorrowe's night ;
If this darke place yet shewe like[1] candle-light,

---

[8] '*light of light*' (2 qu.)—error of repetition for 'light of life' (A and A 1613).

[9] '*whiles*' (Q 1), as beginning a parallel clause with l. 1, is preferable to 'that' of Q 2, A and A 1613.

[1] '*like*': 2 qu. 'by.' Stella, his sun, is absent, and he left in

Some beautie's peece, as amber-colour'd hed, head
Milke hands, rose cheeks, or lips more sweet, more red ;
Or seeing jets² blacke but in blacknesse bright ;
They please, I do confesse they please mine eyes.
But why? because of you they models be ;
Models, such be wood-globes of glist'ring skies.
Deere, therefore be not iealous ouer me,
If you heare that they seeme my heart to moue ;
Not them, O no,³ but you in them I loue.

XCII.
'All said, still say the same.'

BE your words made, good Sir, of Indian ware,
That you allow me them⁴ by so small rate?

night. 'If, therefore,' he continues, ' meaner beauties having some or some one of thy attributes—amber hair, milk hands, black eyes, and the like—show " like " candle-light to me and attract me, understand that they please me as models of thee.' As Stella is his sun, so are they candle-light to him in his darkness. Thence 'like,' not 'by,' is the right word.

² See longer Notes and Illustrations (g) at close.

³ More expressive than ' No, no ' of 2 qu.

⁴ '*mee them*' (A and A 1613) runs better than 'them mee' (2 qu.).

Or do you curtted[5] Spartanes imitate?
Or do you meane my tender eares to spare,
That to my questions you so totall are?
When I demaund of Phœnix-Stella's state,
You say, forsooth, you left her well of late:
O God, thinke you that satisfies my care?
I would know whether she did[6] sit or walke;
How cloth'd; how waited on; sigh'd she, or smilde
Whereof,—with whom,—how often did she talke;
With what pastimes[7] Time's iourney she beguilde;
If her lips daignd to sweeten my poore name.
Saie all; and all well sayd, still say the same.

[5] '*curted*': 'cutted' (Q 2, A and A 1613). The latter does not agree with the sense of the passage nor with Spartan character. But Spartan brevity does: hence, irregular as the word is, I accept 'curted' from A 1605 and later. Q 1 has 'do you the Caconians imitate?'—a misprint for Laconians.

[6] '*did*' (2 qu.), omitted, by error, in A and A 1613: 'do' seems a modern interpolation from ignorance of 2 qu. Similarly, in l. 13, 'daine' of 2 qu. is the several times repeated error of omitting final *d* or *t*, or mistaking it for *e*. Cf. how often did she talk, &c.

[7] '*pastimes*' (2 qu.) is probably correct, and seems better than 'pastime': 'journeys' for 'journey' is more doubtful, unless he took it according to its etymology as = daily courses. I adopt the

XCIII.

'*Tho' worlds 'quite me, shall I my selfe forgiue?*'

O FATE,[8] O fault, O curse, child of my blisse !
What sobs can giue words grace my griefe to
   show ?
What inke is blacke inough to paint my woe ?
Through me—wretch me—euen Stella vexèd is.
Yet, truth—if caitif's breath may[9] call thee—this
Witnesse with me, that my foule stumbling so,
From carelesnesse did in no maner grow ;
But wit, confus'd with too much care, did misse.
And do I, then, my selfe this vaine 'scuse giue ?
I haue[1]—live I, and know this—harmèd thee ;

---

former, refuse the latter. 'Totall' (of l. 5) is a rather curious use
= you tote or sum up my questions in one general and therefore
short and single answer.

[8] '*fate*': A 1605 and later editions read 'faire,' and a pathetic
passionate meaning might underlie the word in relation to the
abrupt 'fault,' 'curse,' &c.

[9] '*may*': 2 qu. 'might'—not so good.

[1] Line 10, '*I haue—liue I and know this!—harmèd thee*' (A
and A 1613): infinitely superior to 2 qu., 'I do sweete Loue'
(= give myself this excuse), a repetition from l. 9, 'and [yet]
know that this harmèd thee.'

Tho'² worlds 'quite me, shall I my selfe forgiue?
Only with paines my paines thus easèd be,
That all thy hurts in my hart's wracke I reede;
I cry thy sighs, my deere, thy teares I bleede.

XCIV.³

'Griefe.'

GRIEFE, find the words; for thou hast made my braine
So darke with misty vapours, which arise
From out thy heauy mould, that inbent eyes
Can scarce discerne the shape of mine owne paine.
Do thou, then—for thou canst—do thou complaine
For my poore soule, which now that sicknesse tries,

---

² '*Tho*'': 2 qu. 'the,' which is not sense: but 'worlds' (A 1613) is deeper and stronger than 'words' (A), and than 'world' (2 qu.).=This alone is his comfort, that his own woes are eased by his adopting and bearing her griefs; his feeling for her griefs deadens his own: 'quite'=acquit.

³ The readings of Q 1, as shown in l. 1 ('vaine' for 'braine'); l. 3 ('euen mine' for 'inbent'); l. 8 ('and of' for 'lodge there'); l. 9 ('The execution of my fate' for our text), and l. 10 ('not vouchsaft' for 'worthy so'), as taken with l. 11, are clearly earlier; but 'wit' (l. 6) must be an error, and probably also in l. 1

Which euen to sence, sence of it selfe denies,
Though harbengers⁴ of death lodge there his traine.
Or if thy loue of plaint yet mine⁵ forbeares,
  As of a caitife worthy so to die;
Yet waile⁶ thy selfe, and waile with causefull teares,
That though in wretchednesse thy life doth lie,
Yet growest more wretched then thy nature beares
  By being placed in such a wretch as I.

XCV.

'*Sighes.*'

YET sighes, deare sighs, indeede true friends you are,
  That do not leaue your left⁷ friend at the wurst,

' vaine,' and not a variant; for the sickness that now tries his, is, as described in ll. 7-8, paralysis, a disease of the brain and spinal cord.

⁴ '*harbengers*' (2 qu.): I prefer this to 'harbenger': 'his' is =death. He is addressing 'grief,' and therefore it must be 'thy loue, not 'the'—just as we have 'wail thyself'=wail thine own case, and 'shewe.'

⁵ '*mine*': 2 qu. 'mind,' error as in MS. Sonnets ii., iii., and A in Sonnets ix. l. 13, for 'mine' (Q 1, A and A 1613)=my plaint or pains. The thought is very forced, and in none of the variations has he succeeded in making ll. 9-10 agree with context.

⁶ '*wail*': 2 qu. grossly misprint 'wave.'

⁷ '*left*': 'best,' Q 1 is a good reading, but 'least' (Q 2), which

But, as you with my breast I oft haue nurst,
So, gratefull now, you waite vpon my care.
Faint coward Ioy no longer tarry dare,
Seeing Hope yeeld when this wo strake him furst;
Delight exclaims he is for my fault curst,[8]
Though oft[9] himselfe my mate in arms he sware;

in itself is nonsense, shows that the original from which it was taken had, like it, 'left,' *i.e.* left by every one else, or desolate: or query—deeper still, a sub-allusion to Stella's having 'left' him (as in Sonnet lxxxvii.). As Q 2 original was different from that of A and A 1613 (see ll. 7-8), the coincidence proves 'left' to be correct, and an author's variant.

[8] Our text (from 2 qu.) is far better than A and A 1613—

'Delight protests he is not for the[e] accurst';

for the essence of the accusation, he sware himself my mate in arms, lies in the defection of this mate, not in his being also 'curst,' a thing that would rather make him a partner of Sidney's fortunes than otherwise. Besides, when Delight is cursed, he is no longer Delight. Of course in favour of A and A 1613 is the consequent that 'curst' he must still be Sidney's mate at arms, and therefore not forsworne, but *sans reproche*. Yet is Q 1 deeper and fuller. Mr. Thomson (as before) prefers the reading of A and A 1613 just as therein, *i.e.* 'the' not 'thee': the meaning being —Delight protests that I am accurst, and that he is not for me or 'for my turn'—a common Elizabethan idiom.

[9] The 'oft' swearing makes the abandonment the greater and more shameful. 2 qu. transpose 'himself' before 'he sware.'

Nay, Sorrow comes with such maine rage, that he
Kils his owne children—teares—finding that they
By Loue were made apt to consort with me.
Only, true sighs, you do not goe away :
Thanke may you haue for such a thankfull part,
Thank-worthiest yet when you shall breake my hart.
                                              [heart

XCVI.

'*Thought.*'

THOUGHT,[1] with good cause thou likest so well
    the night,
Since kind or chance giues both one liverie,[2]
Both sadly blacke, both blackly darkned be ;   [barred
Night bard from sun, thou from thy owne sunlight ;
Silence in both displaies his sullen might ;
Slow heauinesse[3] in both holds one degree—

---

[1] Usually misprinted 'though.'

[2] '*liverie*': 2 qu. misprint 'libertie': and 'kin' for 'kind' is Gray's and modern editors' error.

[3] '*Slowe heauinesse*': 'Low,' Gray's and modern editor's error, and 'heauens' (2 qu.) a misreading for 'heauinesse.' Cf. silence, heaviness, and solitariness, in which they agree. Besides, his 'thought' could not be said to have 'slow heavens,' and there is

That full of doubts, thou of perplexity;
Thy teares expresse Night's natiue moisture right;
In both amazeful[4] solitarinesse:
In night, of sp'rites[5] the gastly powers do stur;[6] ghastly
In thee, or sp'rites or sp'rited gastlinesse.
But, but, alas, Night's side the ods hath fur: far
For that, at length, yet doth inuite some rest;
Thou, though still tired, yet still doost it detest.

no reason why 'slow heavens' should be full of doubt; there is no agreement between 'slow' as applied to the progress of the Night, and 'full of doubt.'

[4] '*amazeful*': far better than 'woefull,' because we have just had tears in the preceding line, and because it had a much stronger sense then than now, agreeing more with its primitive 'maze.' Thus Shakespeare speaks of 'mated and amazed' (*Macbeth*, act v. sc. 1).

[5] '*Sprites*': modern error of punctuation. The construction is, In night stir the ghastly powers of sprites, In thee, &c.

[6] Lines 8-10. Taking the punctuation 'solitariness' (2 qu. and A and A 1613), we must change 'to' (A and A 1613), into 'do,' thus making it agree with 'stur' (Q 2) and 'slurr,' Q 1 (a misprint for 'sturr'), except that A and A 1613 scan 'powers,' and 2 qu. 'pŏwĕrs.' If we read 'solitariness,' then 'to' can stand; but this seems forbidden by 'amazeful' or 'woeful' (2 qu.), which makes l. 9 a separate clause, describing the effect of solitariness on us. I look, however, on A and A 1613 thus altered (viz. 'to' to 'do') as later than 2 qu.; because 'thought'

XCVII.

'Dian's peere.'

DIAN, that faine would cheare her friend the Night,
Shewes her[7] oft, at the full, her fairest face,
Bringing with her those starry nymphs, whose chace[8]
From heauenly standing hits[9] each mortall wight.
But ah, poore Night, in loue with Phœbus' light,
And endlesly dispairing of his grace,
Her selfe—to shewe no other ioy hath place—
Sylent and sad, in mourning weedes doth dight.

being the thing addressed, the change to 'In our sprites' (2 qu.) alters the name, and in some degree the personality, while the idea in A and A 1613, that 'thought' at one time raises up grisly phantoms, and at another is pale with a ghostly ghastliness, is fuller and better than 2 qu.

[7] '*Shewes her*': 2 qu. 'Doth shew'—indifferent.

[8] Lines 3-4, '*chace*' is here used generally for 'hunt,' and he is speaking of that kind of hunting affected by ladies, when the hunters do not follow their game, but move to what is technically called 'their standings,' whence they shot at the passing game (as in *Love's Labour's Lost*).

[9] '*hits*': 2 qu. 'hurts,'—the latter does not express the sense, as does the vaguer 'hits' (A and A 1613), because the allusion is to the effect of the stars on men's destinies. It was only at the close of his life that the stars in their courses fought against Sisera.

Euen so, alas, a lady, Dian's peere,
With choise delights[1] and rarest company
Would faine driue cloudes from out my heavy cheere;
But, wo is me, though Ioy her selfe were she,
Shee could not shew my blind braine waies of ioy,
While I despaire my sunne's sight[2] to enioy.

XCVIII.
'*Loue's Spur.*'

AH, bed! the field where Ioye's peace some do see,
    The field where all my thoughts to warre be train'd,
How is thy grace by my strange fortune strain'd!
How thy lee-shores[3] by my sighes stormèd be!

---

[1] '*delights*' = varied delights, not 'delight' (2 qu.), which is hardly English, except in the sense of delight to her.

[2] 2 qu. 'light'—indifferent.

[3] 2 qu. 'low shroudes':—the latter is a certain error. The shrouds of a vessel are those stays to the mast that are formed into a ladder, and have no analogue in a bed, and neither in a ship nor in the high-canopied beds of those days could any such be called 'low.' Possibly the original 'low or lee stronds'; the sighs storm the bed, to others a refuge, as the winds and waves beat on a restless lee-shore, that is no comfort, but danger, to the tossed mariner.

With sweete soft shades thou oft inuitest me
To steale some rest; but, wretch, I am constrained—
Spurd with Loue's spur, though gald,[4] and shortly
  rain'd   reined
With Care's hard hand—to turne and tosse in thee,
While the blacke horrors of the silent night
Paint Woe's blacke face so liuely to[5] my sight,
That tedious leasure markes each wrinkled line:
But when Aurora leades out Phœbus' daunce,
Mine eyes then only winke; for spite, perchaunce,
That wormes should haue their sun, and I want mine.

XCIX.[6]

'*Sleep's Armory.*'

WHEN far-spent Night perswades each mortall eye,
  To whome nor Art nor Nature graunteth[7] light,

---

[4] '*gald*': sometimes '*gold*'—either makes sense.

[5] '*to*': 2 qu. '*in*': the former preferable, because he looks on Woe's face, and marks each wrinkled line. A 1613 has, badly, '*makes.*'

[6] Several of these later Sonnets are very incorrect in the 2 qu.; the next especially, and the present has some errors.

[7] '*graunteth*': 2 qu. '*granted.*' Night persuades to sleep

VOL. I. I

To lay his then marke-wanting shafts of sight,
Clos'd with their quiuers, in Sleep's armory;
With windowes ope, then most my mind[8] doth lie,
Viewing the shape of darknesse, and delight
Takes in that sad hue, which, with th' inward night
Of his mazde powers, keepes perfet harmony :[9]

those eyes which at that time may have neither material nor artificial light; therefore 'graunteth' (A and A 1613), 'granted' without 'hath,' not only means they were without it at some other time, but were always without light.

[8] '*mind*' (A and A 1613), as preferable to 'heart' (2 qu.). There is no reason why his heart should be viewing the darkness, and the complaint is he lies broad awake. And yet, as Sidney's whole passion was of the 'heart' rather than of the 'mind,' there seems little doubt 'heart' is an Author's variant. In ll. 6-7 the meaning is not that the mind *takes in* that sad hue but *takes delight in* that sad hue.

[9] Lines 7-8. This thought of harmony has been elaborated in Sonnet xcvi., and he says that his wakeful mind looking on the darkness takes in that sad, that visible darkness, with which the inward night of his mazed powers is in perfect harmony. This at once shows 'might' (2 qu.) to be a misreading : Q 2, again, rightly seeing there was no sense in Q 1, when the inward might of his mazed powers kept harmony with the surrounding darkness, made apparently an attempt at sense, by interpolating 'he,'—an attempt which makes the outward sad hue one and the same with the inward might! Lastly, if the inward might of his mind be in

ASTROPHEL AND STELLA. 131

But when birds charme,[1] and that sweete aire which is
Morne's messenger, with rose-enameld skies
Cals each wight to salute the floure[2] of blisse ;
In tombe[3] of lids then buried are mine eyes,
Forst by their lord, who is asham'd to find
Such light in sense, with such a darkned mind.

harmony with the outer darkness, it cannot take its hue from it.
And if it could, and did, it would have done exactly the reverse of
what Sidney would express, and has expressed in Sonnets lxxxix.
xci. xcvi. and xcvii. ; because saying the mind gets dark at dark,
involves the idea that during the day it was lightsome. Therefore 'And takes that' must be rejected for 'Takes in' (A and A 1613);
though the marked want of 'and' or a personal pronoun makes it
very unpleasant to our eares. One would like to think that the
'And' had dropped down from the line above. 'Powres' in Q 1 is
dissyllabic, in Q 2 and A and A 1613 monosyllabic.

[1] '*charme*': 2 qu. ' chirpe.' One cannot accept 'aires'; for the
expression is uncouth, and it would seem to be an accidental
repetition of 'aire,' of 'sweet aire.' The old word 'charme' still
used in Devon, is far more expressive of the pleasant soundings of
their united voices. So too in Scotland still, 'chirm.'

[2] '*floure*': 2 qu. 'heauen' : the latter seems an over-strong term
for either the morning or the morning skies ; and 'floure' seems
an equally over-strong reference to the rose that enamels the skies.
We can only remember that Sidney was a Poet and—a Lover.

[3] '*In tombe*' (A and A 1613) is more like Sidney's style, and that
of his day, than 'intomb'd,' and more accurate grammatically.

C.

'All mirth farewell.'

O TEARES! no teares, but raine,[4] from Beautie's skies,
Making those lillies and those roses growe,
Which ay most faire, now more then most faire show,[5]
While gracefull Pitty Beautie beautifies.
O honied[6] sighs! which from that breast do rise,
Whose pants do make vnspilling creame to flow,
Wing'd with whose breath, so pleasing zephires blow.[7]

---

[4] '*raine*': 2 qu. 'showres'—the latter softer, but 'raine' simpler and preferable.

[5] 2 qu. read 'Which are most faire, now fairer needs must show.'

[6] 'Oh, minded' (2 qu.), 'sighted' (Q 1), are errors—the latter for 'sigh'd,' as changed in A and A 1613 to 'sobbed'—deeper and better: and while we can in l. 4 understand how 'graceful Pity beautifies Beauty' (A and A 1613), it is impossible to understand why Pity should be 'grateful' (2 qu.).

[7] 2 qu. 'Winged with woe's breath, so doth Zephire blow.' This does not scan; or else makes with 'wingèd' an unrhythmical length of ten syllables. Again, while 'Woe's breath' (2 qu.) is a strange refresher in Hell, Sidney's after-use of 'pleasing' (A and A 1613) shows that the transcriber's mind—thinking of 'plaints' and 'sighs'—confusedly transformed 'whose' into 'woe's.'

As might[8] refresh the hell where my soule fries.
O plaints ! conseru'd in such a sugred phrase,
That Eloquence itself enuies your praise,
While sobd-out words a perfect musike giue.
Such teares, sighs, plaints, no sorrow is, but ioy :
Or if such heauenly signes must proue annoy,
All mirth farewell, let me in sorrow liue.

CI.

'Stella is sicke.'

STELLA is sicke, and in that sicke-bed lies
   Sweetnesse, which breathes and pants as oft as she :
And Grace, sicke too, such fine conclusion tries,
That Sickenesse brags it selfe best graced to be.
Beauty is sicke, but sicke in so[9] faire guise,
That in that palenesse Beautie's white we see ;
And Ioy, which is inseparate from those eyes,
Stella, now learnes, strange case, to weepe in me.[1]

---

[8] '*might*' (2 qu.) : better and deeper than 'can' (A and Λ 1613), with a touch of pathos in it.

[9] Sonnet ci. l. 5, '*so*' : Sidney's usual word : better than 'such' (2 qu.).

[1] The thought is very forced, but joy being inseparable from

Loue mones thy paine,[2] and like a faithfull page,
As thy lookes sturre, runs[3] vp and downe, to make
All folkes prest at thy will thy paine to swage ;
Nature with care sweates for her darling's sake,
Knowing worlds passe, ere she enough can finde,
Of such heauen-stuffe to cloath so heauenly a minde.

Stella's eyes, she could weep 'in it' (A and A 1613), but not 'with it' (2 qu.) ; for that involves joy weeping for grief. Hence the reading cannot be 'with thee.' 'With me' (2 qu.) gives a sort of sense, but probably a transcriber's rather than the Author's. We must then read joy as = O Joy,—an apostrophe to joy, and 'which .... eyes' as an interjectional clause. This introduces a thought wholly foreign to the rest of the Sonnet, which shows how Stella's sweetness, grace, beauty and joy—all inherent iñ her—behaved during her sickness. Her eyes, says Sidney, were always a bright joy to others, and still are a joy, though they weep. 2 qu. 'vnseuered' for 'inseparate' (A and A 1613). Mr. Thomson (as before) writes :—The comma after Stella is not in 1623 edⁿ. If there is good authority for it, I would explain ll. 7-8 thus—"Your eyes cannot but give me joy, but now (because of your sickness) that joy is learning to weep." Without the comma, the meaning would be, " Stella's eyes cannot but give me joy, but Stella in her present state learns, *i.e.* teaches, that joy to weep."

² See longer Notes and Illustrations (*h*) at close.

³ '*runs*' (2 qu.) seems better than 'comes' (A and A 1613), and so, l. 11, 'swage' than 'asswage' : but l. 12, 'seekes' (2 qu.), has nothing that she seeks for, and 'sweates' (A and A 1613) not unlikely refers to the perspirations which relieved the febrile state.

CII.

'It is but loue.'

WHERE be those roses gone,[4] which sweetned so
    our eyes?[5]
Where those red cheeks, which oft, with faire encrease,
    did frame
The[6] height of honour in the kindly badge of shame?
Who hath the crimson weeds stolne from my[7] morning
    skies?

---

[4] In 2 qu. reads inferiorly 'Where be those roses which so sweetned our eyes?'—unrhythmical, and less expressive than our text (A and A 1613).

[5] In 2 qu. reads 'Where be those red cheekes, which faire increase did frame?' won't scan or make sense: 'with' was probably omitted; but as the talk is of blushing, and as Stella was not always blushing 'oft' (A and A 1613) is far better than 'be' (2 qu.): 'did' (2 qu., A and A 1613): 'doth,' a mistake of A 1605.

[6] '*The*': 2 qu. 'No'—a ludicrous mistake, completely reversing the sense, which is, that in the kindly (or natural) badge of shame, *i.e.* the blush, she shows honour's height; in other words, her blushes are chaste blushes, the tokens of a chaste love.

[7] '*my.*' The crimson weeds had been stolen from his morning skies, from Stella's face now pale: 'the' (2 qu.) would imply the reverse, that Stella had stolen crimson from the skies.

How doth the colour vade[8] of those vermilion dies,
Which Nature' selfe did make, and self-ingrain'd the
    same?
I would know by what right this palenesse ouercame
That hue, whose force my hart still unto[9] thraldome
    ties?
Galen's adoptiue[1] sonnes, who by a beaten way
Their iudgements hackney on, the fault of[2] sicknesse
    lay;
But feeling proofe[3] makes me say they mistake it furre:

[8] '*vade*' (A and A 1613) is here the right word, not 'fade' (2 qu.). See note in SOUTHWELL, *s. v.*: 'eies' (2 qu.), the most preposterous error in the book, Nature making Stella ferret-eyed, and being praised for it; and more, the loss of their vermillion-hue gravely asserted and plaintively lamented. Further to increase these absurdities, Nature, in l. 9, 'engraued' this redness. See note on 'grain,' in Sonnet lxxx.

[9] '*still unto*': *i.e.* though absent, it yet has force—far preferable, therefore, to 'in so great' (2 qu.).

[1] '*adoptiue*,'—better than 'adopted' (2 qu.), which seems to say that Galen, dead for centuries, had adopted them.

[2] '*of*.' The fault is paleness and absence of red, so that 'as' (A and A 1613) seems better; but 'of' (2 qu.) is undoubtedly the favourite particle with Sidney: accepted.

[3] '*proofe*'(2 qu. and A 1613): 'pulse' (A), Author's variants: feeling = sympathising. 'Feeling the pulse' is used in 'Certain

It is but loue which makes this paper perfit white,
To write therein more fresh the storie of delight,
Whiles Beautie's reddest inke Venus for him doth sturre.

CIII.

'Golden Haire.'

O HAPPIE Thames, that didst my Stella beare !
I saw thee with full many a smiling line
Vpon thy cheerefull face, Ioye's liuery[4] weare,
While those faire planets on thy streames did shine.
The boate for ioy could not to daunce forbear,
While wanton winds, with beauties[5] so diuine
Rauisht, staid not, till in her golden haire
They did themselues, O[6] sweetest prison, twine.

Sonnets,' as see in the place noted: 'furre' stronger and better than 'sure' (2 qu.). Sidney uses this rhyme 'fur' and 'stur' in Sonnet xcvi. A and A 1613 make the blunder of putting 'say they' in ( ), thus reversing the sense.

[4] *'Ioye's livery'* (A and A 1613), better, as proved by ll. 1, 2, 3 and 5, than 'Loue's.'

[5] *'beauties'*=all her several beauties : he has just spoken of her eyes: better than 'beauty' (2 qu.).

[6] 'O' is dropped by error in 2 qu.—required by metre.

And[7] faine those Æol's youth there would their stay
Haue made, but forst by Nature still to flie,
First did with puffing kisse those lockes display:
She, so disheuld[8] blusht: from window I   dishevelled
With sight thereof cride out, 'O[9] faire disgrace,
Let Honor' selfe to thee grant highest place.'

CIV.

'Enuious wits.'

ENUIOUS wits, what hath bene mine offence,
   That with such poysonous[10] care my lookes you
     marke,
That to each word, nay sigh of mine, you harke,
As grudging me my sorrowe's eloquence?
Ah, is it not enough, that I am thence,
Thence, so farre thence, that scantly any sparke
Of comfort dare come to this dungeon darke,

---

[7] '*And*': 2 qu. '*But*': out of place, and 'but' is in the next line: 'friendly words' (2 qu.), poor, when he has just said 'wanton winds.'

[8] '*disheueld*': 2 qu. '*discouered*'—perhaps indifferent, but the former the later, as shown by l. 9.

[9] '*O*,' more appropriate than 'ah' (2 qu.).

[10] 'Line 2, '*poysonous*' (A 1613) = malevolent, empoisoned,

Where Rigour's exile lockes vp al my sense?
But if I by a happie window passe,
If I but stars vppon mine armour beare;
Sicke, thirsty, glad¹ (though but of empty glasse):
Your morall² notes straight my hid meaning teare
From out my ribs, and, puffing, proues that I³
Doe Stella loue : fooles, who doth it deny?

hence 'poisoned' of 2 qu. : 'wits' (2 qu.) probably an error by repetition for 'lookes.'

¹ The meaning is, If I am glad to have even the empty glass which should contain the wine of beauty for which I thirst.

² '*morall*' (A and A 1605) : 'mortall,' error of A 1613, &c.

³ Lines 12-13. There has been an attempt to make sense of the error of 2 qu. in l. 12 by putting (,) after there, and it succeeds in giving some sense, though strange English, to that line. Line 13, however, becomes nonsensical, and remains nonsense, if we take away (,), and this makes nonsense also of l. 12 : for who ever heard of noting a man's meaning out of his ribs, especially when it was the joy in his face and the stars on his armour that they saw? 2 qu. read for 'and, puffing '—' a whirlewind.' On l. 8 be it remarked, that Sidney does not mean that he had left, or that Stella had, but merely that he was debarred her presence. The presence of the wits, and the mention of tilting-armour, shows he was in some populous place, and it can hardly be doubted, especially if one has regard to the previous sonnets, that he was at Court. It is also clear that Stella was there, by the

CV.

'*Unhappie.*'

UNHAPPIE sight, and hath shee vanisht by
    So nere, in so good time, so free a place!
Dead glasse,[4] dost thou thy obiect so imbrace,
As what my hart still sees thou canst not spie!   heart
I sweare by her I loue and lacke, that I
Was not in fault, who bent thy dazling race
Onely vnto the heau'n of Stella's face,
Counting but dust what in the way did lie.

mention of the happy window. The ensuing song, or serenade, confirms this, that she was present, and yet—by a rule she had laid down both for herself and him—absent. See next sonnet and notes.

[4] This sonnet recounts his endeavour to see Stella as she passed on a dark night, and confirms the view taken of the preceding sonnet. The 'dead glasse' is a telescope, and it is obvious the words must be 'thy dazling race' (A and A 1613), not 'my' (2 qu.), and l. 8, '*the* way'=the telescope's line of sight, not 'her' (2 qu.), Stella's way. In l. 6 'who' (A and A 1613) better than 'that' (2 qu.), and l. 8 'what' (*ib.*) than 'that' (2 qu.) Line 6, 'I loue and lacke' is, under the tenant (*i.e.* one in place of the general-in-chief, as Cassio was Othello's lieutenant) commands more than one, and we have 'powers' (l. 2) therefore 'thoughts,' not 'thought.'

ASTROPHEL AND STELLA. 141

But cease, mine eyes, your teares do witnesse well
That you, guiltlesse thereof,[5] your nectar mist :
Curst be the page from whome the bad torch fell :
Curst be the night which did your strife[6] resist :
Curst be the coachman that[7] did driue so fast,
With[8] no lesse curse then absence makes me tast.

[5] '*thereof*' (A and A 1613) : 'therefore' (2 qu.)—either, according to the old use of therefore, will suit. 'Nectar' (A and A 1613) : 'necklace' (2 qu.)—the latter may be an early variant and refer to some gift of his ; but it is lack of seeing her that he bemoans, and hence is hardly likely to have mentioned a mere necklace, even if he had given Stella one ; and if he did, he wisely altered it. If the conjectures in the note on the Sonnet are correct (l. 6), he could not anticipate that she would necessarily wear a gift of his.

[6] '*your strife*' (A and A 1613) : 'your will' (2 qu.). Both refer to her eyes using the telescope rather than, perhaps, the telescope itself. The word 'strife' [with darkness] is much more expressive.

[7] '*that*' (2 qu.) reads better than 'which' (A and A 1613).

[8] '*which*' is error of later A for 'With' (2 qu., A and A 1605, 1613) : and these later also have 'whence' for 'whane,' l. 11 : 'lesse' (2 qu.), 'worse' (A and A 1613). Though by adopting a subtlety of thought = my curse in not seeing her is so great that I can wish him no worse in kind—this latter gives a similar sense with 'lesse,' it is not so good as it.

CVI.

'Absent presence.'

O ABSENT presence ! Stella is not here ;
    False-flattering hope, that with so faire a face
Bare me in hand, that in this orphane place,
Stella, I say[9] my Stella, should appeare :
What saist thou now ? where is that dainty cheere
Thou told'st[1] mine eyes should helpe their famisht case ?
But thou art gone,[2] now that selfe-felt disgrace
Doth make me most to wish thy comfort neere.
But heere I do store of faire ladies meete,
Who may with charme of conuersation sweete
Make in my heauy mould new thoughts to grow.
Sure they preuaile as much with me, as he
That bad his friend, but then new maim'd to be   bade
Mery with him, and so forget his woe.[3]

---

[9] '*say*': 2 qu. '*saw*,'—an error; as '*cleare*' (*ib.*) for '*cheare*' (l. 5).

[1] '*toldst*' (A and A 1613), 2 qu. '*would'st*': the former demanded by '*false-flattering*' (l. 2) and '*rest.*'

[2] '*But how art thou*' (2 qu.) : probably in transcript '*But thou art now*' ('*now*' for '*gone*'), and transposed in the endeavour to make sense of the phrase itself, though nonsense as regards the rest.

[3] With all their blunders in this sonnet, the reading of '*and

CVII.

'See what it is to loue.'

STELLA, since thou so right a princesse art
    Of all the powers which life bestowes on me,
    That ere by them ought vndertaken be,
They first resort vnto that soueraigne part;
Sweete, for a while[4] giue respite to my heart,
    Which pants as though it stil should leape to thee:
    And on my thoughts[5] giue thy lieuetenancie
To this great cause, which needes both use[6] and art.
And as a queene, who from her presence sends
Whom she imployes, dismisse from thee my wit,

so forget his' (2 qu.), which in reality is that also of Q 1, seems better, and is perhaps later, than A and A 1613, 'and not thinke of.'

[4] '*while*': 'time' (2 qu.)—indifferent.

[5] '*thoughts*': 'thought' (2 qu.): a lieutenant (*i.e.* one in place of the general-in-chief, as Cassio was Othello's lieutenant) commands more than one, and we have 'powers' (l. 2); therefore 'thoughts,' not 'thought.'

[6] '*use*': 'wit' (2 qu.) was probably the original word (see l. 10); but it is the lieutenant who should 'use' wit; and besides, 'wit' seems to deprive Stella's 'art' of wisdom: hence 'use,' his thoughts being the soldiers practised in work and trained to obey.

Till[7] it have wrought what thy owne will attends.
On seruants' shame oft maister's blame doth sit :[8]
O, let not fooles in me thy workes reproue,[9]
And scorning say, 'See what it is to loue !'

CVIII.

'*Rude Despaire.*'

WHEN Sorrow (vsing mine owne fier's might)
Melts downe his lead into my boyling brest,
Through that darke furnace to[1] my hart opprest,
There shines a ioy from thee my only light :

---

[7] Error of 'still' (2 qu.) for 'Till' (A and A 1613) seems to have led to further error of 'to' for 'it,' as in Sonnet cvi. l. 7: 'haue' (2 qu., A and A 1613) : 'hath' modern reading.

[8] From what precedes, the thought evidently is [Do this, for] servants' shame doth bring masters' blame, *i.e.* is often cause of blame to the masters : the masters are often blamed for the servants' errors, and so might you be for mine. This is only given by 'On .... sit' (A and A 1613), not 'For.' The next clause is a different thought, My works are all done under your influence, and if you take not this order, my unregulated doings will be a scorn.

[9] '*reproue*': 2 qu. 'approve'—error which reverses the real meaning.

[1] '*to*' (A and A 1613) : 'of' (2 qu.). Both seem at first sight

But soone as thought of thee breeds my delight,
And my yong soule flutters to thee² his nest,
Most rude³ Despaire, my daily 'vnbidden guest,
Clips streight my wings, streight wraps me in his night,
And makes me then bow downe my heade, and say,
Ah, what doth Phœbus' gold that wretch auaile

admissible ; but looking to the phrase 'sorrow weighs down the heart,' and to its being Sorrow's lead that is here spoken of, I take it that the dark furnace is his boiling breast, and that the lead is poured into the heart opprest. If the 'heart' be the 'furnace,' as it must be with 'of,' then are the 'fires' in the heart; and besides that such an idea is rather incongruous with the intended thought, Sidney has markedly divided the one from the other. The 'dark furnace' was so called, perhaps, with reference to the dark flames of Hell—a philosophy then common, and afterwards adopted by Milton. Mr. Thomson (as before) writes :—
"a ray of joy from Stella penetrates through that dark furnace into my heart. The furnace is of course his breast, and it is dark because the heat is produced by boiling water and molten lead, neither of which is luminous."

² '*flutters to thee*' (A and A 1613) explains what is not otherwise explained, who or what is the 'nest.' 'His' (*ib.*) is also more appropriate than 'her' (2 qu.), as the love of a male for a female is in question.

³ (A and A 1613): 2 qu. 'dead.' The text is preferable, as shewn by 'daily vnbidden.'

VOL. I.　　　　　K

Whom iron doores[4] doe keepe from vse of day ?
So strangely, 'alas, thy works in[5] me preuaile,
That in my woes for thee thou art my ioy,
And in my ioyes for thee my onely[6] 'anoy.

CIX.

'*Desire.*'[7]

THOU blind man's marke, thou foole's selfe-chosen snare,
Fond fancie's scum, and dregs of scattered thought :
Band of all euils ; cradle of causelesse care ;

---

[4] 2 qu. 'darts'—error.   [5] (A and A 1613): 2 qu. 'on'—error.
[6] (A and A 1613), and punctuated 'onely,' which is clearly what is meant by 'onel 'anoy,' of 2 qu.
[7] Sonnets cix. and cx. I refer to our Essay, as before, for reasons that constrained me to place these two Sonnets, cix. and cx., as the fitting, and by the Author the intended, close of Astrophel and Stella. They are interpenetrated with passion, but a passion that recognises how idle and misdirected such love as he has been dallying with is—and so he closes his Sonnets. 'Grow rich,' of cx. l. 3, is not an accidental use of the word 'rich.' Usually at the end of this last sonnet there is added, as with us, the Latin motto, 'Splendidis longum valedico nugis,' which gathers into itself fresh significance as belonging to the close of Astrophel and Stella ; otherwise is meaningless.

Thou web of will, whose end is neuer wrought :
Desire ! Desire ! I haue too dearly bought,
With prise of mangled mind, thy worthlesse ware ;
Too long, too long, asleepe thou hast me brought,
Who shouldst my mind to higher things prepare.
But yet in vaine thou hast my ruine sought ;
In vaine thou madest me to vaine things aspire ;
In vaine thou kindlest all thy smokie fire ;
For Vertue hath this better lesson taught,—
Within myselfe to seeke my onelie hire,
Desiring nought but how to kill Desire.

CX.

'Aspire to higher things.'

LEAUE me, O Loue, which reachest but to dust ;
And thou, my mind, aspire to higher things ;
Grow rich in that which never taketh rust ;
Whateuer fades, but fading pleasure brings.
Draw in thy beames, and humble all thy might
To that sweet yoke where lasting freedomes be ;
Which breakes the clowdes, and opens forth the light,
That doth both shine, and giue us sight to see.
O take fast hold ; let that light be thy guide

In this small course which birth drawes out to death,
And thinke how euill becommeth him to slide,
Who seeketh heau'n, and comes of heau'nly breath.
Then farewell, world; thy vttermost I see:
Eternall Loue, maintaine thy life in me.

Splendidis Longum Valedico Nugis.

SONGS

IN

ASTROPHEL AND STELLA.

SONGS.

The whole of these are verses which by their construction, even if there were no proofs such as may be found in the first and last stanzas of the first song, and the closing stanza of the eleventh, were clearly set to music and sung. Hence they are more properly Songs, and are so called in A and A 1613, though headed 'Sonets' in 2 qu. I have brought them together here rather than interspersed them among the Sonnets, as in A and A 1613, but not originally (*e.g.* 2 qu.), because they interrupt the thought and study of the sonnets, and because they form an entirely different type of poetry. But see our Essay, for a critical examination of the inter-relations of Sonnets and Songs.

G.

FIRST SONG.[1]

1. DOÚBT yóu to whom my Muse these notes
   enténdeth,
   Which nów my breast, surcharg'd,[2] to musick
   lendeth !
   To you, to you, all song of praise is due,
   Only in you my song begins and endeth.

---

[1] There is a mistake running through all A and the greater part of 2 qu. The first two lines of each stanza are questions or questioning exclamations, and require (?) or (!). I have placed (!). In line 3 the 2 qu. often substitute ' be ' for ' is,' but there are no changes in sense or construction which require this change, and ' is ' is the stronger word.

[2] '*surcharg'd.*' Sidney did not certainly affect French words, and in the last stanza, which is a repetition of this, 2 qu. and A and A 1613 have ' orecharged.' Still I accept the singularly passionate and expressively full word ' surcharg'd ' of 2 qu. here. 2 qu. badly misprint ' with ' music, which makes Sidney guilty unnecessarily of self-laudation. A = he lends (or in other phrase marries) to music the words of his surcharg'd breast.

II. Who hath the eyes which marrie state with pleasure!
Who keeps the key of Nature's chiefest treasure!
To you, to you, all song of praise is due,
Only for you the heau'n forgate³ all measure.

III. Who hath the lips, where wit in fairenesse raigneth!
Who womankind at once both deckes and stayneth!⁴
To you, to you, all song of praise is due,
Onely by you Cupid his crowne maintaineth.

IV. Who hath the feet, whose step all⁵ sweetnesse planteth!
Who else, for whom Fame worthy trumpets wanteth!

---

³ '*forgate*,' *i.e.* in past tense=when they made her. Better than 2 qu. 'forget.'

⁴ '*stayneth*'=stains other womankind by comparison. Her 'passing ['surpassing'] fairenesse' makes that of others ugliness.

⁵ '*all*.' Nothing is planted, and hence I read with 2 qu. 'all' for 'of,' A and A 1613. But as 'planteth' is singular, with A and A 1613 retain 'step' (=steps collectively), not 'steps.'

To you, to you, all song of praise is due,
Onely to you her scepter Venus granteth.

v. Who hath the breast, whose milk doth patience [6] nourish !
Whose grace is such, that when it chides doth cherish !
To you, to you, all song of praise is due,
Onelie through you the tree of life doth flourish.

vi. Who hath the hand which, without stroke, subdueth !
Who long-dead[7] beautie with increase reneueth !
To you, to you, all song of praise is due,
Onely at you all enuie hopelesse rueth.[8]

vii. Who hath the haire, which, loosest,[9] fastest tieth !
Who makes a man liue, then glad when he dieth !

---

[6] '*patience.*' A and A 1613 read ' passions.' The thought seems obscure, but ' patience,' 2 qu., is clearer than ' passions ' : adopted.

[7] '*long-dead*': stronger than ' long-hid ' of 2 qu., and agrees better with ' renew.'

[8] '*rueth*': 2 qu. badly ' endeth,' which does not rhyme.

[9] '*loosest . . . . fastest*' read better than ' -eth.' 2 qu.

To you, to you, all song of praise is due,
Only of you the flatterer neuer lieth.

VIII. Who hath the voyce, which soule from sences sunders !
Whose force, but yours, the bolts[1] of beautie thunders !
To you, to you, all song of praise is due,
Only with you not[2] miracles are wonders.

IX. Doubt you, to whome my Muse these notes intendeth,
Which now my breast, orecharged, to musicke lendeth !
To you, to you, all song of praise is due :
Only in you my song begins and endeth.

---

[1] '*bolts.*' Both sense and our English idiom require 'bolts' rather than 'bolt,' 2 qu.—the latter probably a conjectural or accidental change, due to 'thunders' in singular.

[2] '*not*': better than 'no' (2 qu.) = wonders are not miracles.

SECOND SONG.[3]

I. HAUE I caught my heau'nly iewell,
Teaching Sleepe most faire to be!
Now will I teach her that she,
When she wakes, is too-too cruell.

II. Since sweet Sleep her eyes hath charmèd,
The two only darts of Loue,
Now will I, with that Boy, proue,
Some play, while he is disarmèd.

III. Her tongue, waking, still refuseth,
Giuing frankly niggard no :
Now will I attempt to know
What no her tongue, sleeping, vseth.

IV. See the hand that, waking, gardeth,   guardeth
Sleeping, grants a free resort :
Now will I inuade the fort,
Cowards Loue with losse rewardeth.

---

[3] i. l. 1. Falstaff adopts this in his feigned ecstasy at meeting Mistress Ford: 'Have I caught thee, my heavenly jewel?' My

v. But, O foole, thinke of the danger
Of her iust and high disdaine;
Now will I, alas, refraine;
Loue feares nothing else but anger.

vi. Yet those lips, so sweetly swelling,
Do inuite a stealing kisse.
Now will I but venture this;
Who will reade, must first learne spelling.

vii. Oh, sweet kisse! but ah, she's waking;
Lowring beautie chastens me:
Now will I for feare hence flee;
Foole, more foole, for no more taking.[4]

---

good friend the late Mr. Howard Staunton strangely suggested (in his Shakespeare) that Falstaff sang this, as an explanation of 'thee' interpolated, *i.e.* by the players. Their singing would be rather a reason against the interpolation surely.

[4] '*Fool! more fool*' = Fool for running away, more fool for not taking more, *i.e.* not a single kiss, but kisses. Cf. Sonnet lxxiii. &c.

THIRD SONG.[5]

1. IF Orpheus' voyce had force to breathe such musick's loue
Through pores of senceles trees, as it could make them moue;
If stones good measure daunc'd, the Theban walles to build
To cadence of the tunes which Amphion's lyre did yeeld;
More cause a like effect at least-wise bringeth :
O stones, O trees, learne hearing,—Stella singeth.

11. If loue might sweet'n so a boy of shepheard[6] brood,
To make a lyzard dull, to taste loue's dainty[7] food ;
If eagle fierce could so in Grecian mayde delight,

---

[5] See note on relative Sonnet.
[6] 'shepheard' : better and more usual than ' 's,' 2 qu.
[7] ' dainty' : 2 qu. badly drop this word. The construction is—
to make a dull lizard taste, &c. ' This story, and such-like, give great colour of truth to that which Democritus reporteth, namely, Thoas in Arcadia saued his life by means of a dragon. This Thoas being but a very childe, had loued this dragon when he was but young, very well, and nourished him ; but at last, being somewhat fearfull of his nature, and not well knowing his qualities,

As her eyes were his light,[8] her death his endlesse night,—
Earth gaue that loue; heav'n, I trow, loue refineth,—
O birds, O beasts, looke loue,—lo,[9] Stella shineth.

and fearing withal the bignes that now he was growne vnto, had carried him into the mountains and deserts; wherein it fortuned that he was afterward set vpon and invironed by theeves, whereupon he cried out, and the dragon knowing his voice, came forth and rescued him.' Holland's *Pliny*, N. H. l. viii. c. 17 : cf. *Ælian.* l. vi. c. 63.

[8] '*As her eyes were his light,*' 2 qu. : better than 'As his light was her eyes.' 'There hapned a marvellous example about the city Sestos of an Egle; for which in those parts there goes a great name of an egle, and highly is she honored there. A yong maid had brought vp a yong egle by hand : the egle again to requite her kindnes would first, when she was but little, flie abroad a birding, and euer bring part of that shee had gotten vnto her said nurse. In processe of time being grown bigger and stronger, would set vpon wild beasts also in the forrest, and furnish her yong mistresse continually with store of venison. At length it fortuned that the damosell died; and when her funerall fire was set a burning, the egle flew into the mids of it, and there was consumed into ashes with the corps of the said virgin. For which cause, and in memoriall thereof, the inhabitants of Sestos and the parts there adjoyning, erected in that very place a stately monument, such as they call Heroum, dedicated in the name of Jupiter and the virgin, for that the egle is a bird consecrated vnto that god.' Pliny, N. H. l. x. c. 5.

[9] ii. l. 6, 'lo' : preferable to 'for,' 2 qu.

III. The beasts, birds,[10] stones, and trees feele this, and,
    feeling, loue ;
And if the trees nor stones stirre not the same to
    proue,
Nor beasts nor birds do come vnto this blessèd
    gaze,
Know that small loue is quicke, and great loue
    doth amaze ;
They are amaz'd, but you with reason armed,
O eyes, O eares of men, how are you charmed !

FOURTH SONG.

I. ONELY Ioy, now here you are,
    Fit to heare and ease my care,
Let my whispering voyce obtaine
Sweete reward for sharpest paine ;[1]
Take me to thee, and thee to mee :
' No, no, no, no, my Deare, let bee.'

---

[10] '*beasts, birds*,' 2 qu.—this keeps the sequence given in the previous lines : A and A 1613 ' Birds, beasts.'

[1] '*pain*' countenances 'reward,' A and A 1613, rather than rewards,' 2 qu.

II. Night hath closde all in her cloke,
    Twinkling starres loue-thoughts prouoke,
    Danger hence, good care doth keepe,
    Iealouzie himselfe[2] doth sleepe;
    Take me to thee, and thee to mee:
    ' No, no, no, no, my Deare, let bee.'

III. Better place no wit can finde,
    Cupid's knot[3] to loose or binde;
    These sweet flowers our[4] fine bed too,
    Vs in their best language woo:
    Take me to thee, and thee to mee:
    ' No, no, no, no, my Deare, let bee.'

IV. This small light the moone bestowes
    Serues thy beames but[5] to disclose;
    So to raise my hap[6] more hie,

---

[2] '*himself*,' 2 qu.: better than 'itselfe,' A and A 1616, albeit Jealousy is not = Lord Rich, for stanza vii. shows Stella was away from home, *i.e.* from Lord Rich.

[3] '*knot*,' 2 qu.: better than 'yoke,' A and A 1613, which is not appropriate.   [4] '*our*,' better than 'on,' A and A 1613.

[5] '*but*,' A and A 1613: 'for,' 2 qu., badly.

[6] '*hap*' = good luck: 'heart,' 2 qu., gives a doubtful sense.

Feare not else, none can vs spie;
Take me to thee, and thee to mee:
'No, no, no, no, my Deare, let bee.'

v. That you heard was but a mouse,
Dumbe Sleepe holdeth all the house:
Yet asleepe, me thinkes they say,
Yong fooles[7] take time while you may;
Take me to thee, and thee to mee:
'No, no, no, no, my Deare, let bee.'

vi. Niggard time threates, if we misse
This large offer of our blisse,
Long stay, ere he[8] graunt the same:
Sweet, then, while ech thing doth frame,[9]
Take me to thee, and thee to mee:
'No, no, no, no, my Deare, let bee.'

---

[7] '*fooles*,' 2 qu.—gayer and yet deeper than 'folks' of A and A 1613, which is commonplace.

[8] '*he*': 2 qu. 'she'; but Time is never feminine.

[9] '*frame*'=design or build up [it, the time or opportunity].

VII. Your faire mother is a-bed,
   Candles out and curtaines spread ;
   She thinkes you do letters write ;
   Write, but first let me endite ;
   Take me to thee, and thee to mee :
   'No, no, no, no, my Deare, let bee.'

VIII. Sweete, alas, why striue you thus ?
   Concord better fitteth vs ;
   Leaue to Mars the force of hands,
   Your power in your beautie stands ;
   Take thee[1] to me, and me to thee :
   'No, no, no, no, my Deare, let bee.'

IX. Wo to mee, and do you sweare
   Me to hate? but I forbeare ;   unless
   Cursèd be my destines all,   destinies
   That brought me so high to fall ;
   Soone with my death I will please thee :
   'No, no, no, no, my Deare, let bee.'

---

[1] I adopt the transposition of 'thee' and 'me,' made by A and A 1613 against 2 qu. in this stanza only. 'Take me' is contradictory to the previous four lines ; so he says, Do nothing, agree ; take thee to me.

FIFT SONG.

I. WHILE fauour fed my hope, delight with hope was brought,
Thought waited on delight, and speech did follow thought;
Then grew[2] my tongue and pen records vnto thy glory,
I thought all words were lost that were not spent of thee,
I thought each place was darke but where thy lights would be,
And all eares worse then deafe that heard not out thy storie.

II. I said thou wert[3] most faire, and so indeed thou art;
I said thou wert most sweet, sweet poison to my heart;

---

[2] '*grew*': 2 qu. 'drew'—the former stronger, being = tongue and pen became, not merely drew, records.

[3] '*wert*,' 2 qu.: better than 'art,' which seems an error of A and A 1613.

I said my soule was thine, O that[4] I then had
        lyed ;
I said thine eyes were starres, thy breast the milk'n
        way,
Thy fingers Cupid's shafts, thy voyce the angels'
        lay :
And all I[5] said so well, as no man it denied.

III. But now that hope is lost, vnkindnesse kils de-
        light ;
Yet thought and speech do liue, though[6] meta-
        morphos'd quite,
For rage now rules the raines which guided were
        by pleasure ;
I thinke now of thy faults, who late thought[7] of
        thy praise,

---

[4] '*that*': 2 qu. 'would'—former more alliterative and probably later.

[5] '*I . . . . as*': 2 qu. 'is . . . . that'—former better, because it is all 'I said,' and because 'is' is a wrong tense. The error from reduplication of 's' of 'said.' 'As' more alliterative than 'that.'

[6] '*though*': 2 qu. misprint 'thought'; for not thought only, but thought and speech both live and were metamorphosed.

[7] '*thought*': 2 qu. 'wrote'—former better, because he is here

That speech falles now to blame, which did thy
    honour raise,
The same key ope'n can, which can locke up a
    treasure.

IV. Then thou,[8] whom partiall heauens conspir'd in
    one to frame
The proofe of Beautie's worth,[9] th' inheritrix of
    fame,
The mansion seat[1] of blisse, and iust excuse of
    louers ;
See now those feathers pluckt, wherewith thou
    flewest most high :
See what cloudes of reproch shall dark thy hon-
    our's skie :
Whose[2] owne fault cast him downe hardly high
    state recouers.

---

writing of thinking, and in l. 5 of speaking: cf. l. 2 and ll. 4-5 :
and because one may think one way, and write another.

[8] '*Then thou*,' 2 qu.: '*Thou then*,' A and Λ 1613—former accepted.

[9] '*worth*': 2 qu. 'worke'; error, as in DONNE. So 'inheritance' for 'inheritrix.'

[1] '*state*,' 2 qu.: A and Λ 1613 'seat'—latter accepted.

[2] 2 qu. read ' Whom fault once casteth downe '—is ambiguous, for it might mean the fault of some one else cast the sufferer down.

V. And, O my Muse, though oft you luld her in your
    lap,
And then a heau'nly child, gaue her ambrosian
    pap,
And to that braine of hers your kindest[3] gifts
    infused ;
Since she, disdaining me, doth you in me disdaine,
Suffer not her to laugh, while[4] both we suffer paine.
Princes in subiects' wrong must deeme themselves
    abused.

VI. Your client, poore my selfe, shall Stella handle so!
Reuenge ! reuenge ! my Muse ! defiance' trumpet
    blow ;[5]
Threat'n what may be done, yet do more then you
    threaten ;[6]

---

[3] 'kindest,' better than 'highest,' 2 qu.—the Muse being the person and nurse.

[4] 'while,' far better than 'and' of 2 qu.

[5] I follow the 2 qu. construction, making 'Defiance' a genitive : not 'Revenge ....Muse. Defiance trumpet.' 'Revenge, revenge!' and 'Vindicta, vindicta!' were known phrases. But for (,,) I substitute (! !).

[6] There has been a great alteration here, and probably by the Author. The playful mock rage seems to prove A and A 1613

Ah, my sute granted is, I feele my breast doth
swell ;
Now, child, a lesson new you shall begin to spell,
Sweet babes must babies haue, but shrewd gyrles
must be beat'n. dolls

VII. Thinke now no more to heare of warme fine-
odour'd snow,⁷
Nor blushing lillies, nor pearles' ruby-hidden row,
Nor of that golden sea, whose waues in curles are
brok'n ;
But of thy soule, so⁸ fraught with such vngratefulnesse,
As where thou soone might'st helpe, most faith
dost⁹ most oppresse ;
Vngratefull, who is cald, the worst of euils¹ is
spok'n ;

(our text) to be the later. 'Threaten, and do more than you threaten,' agrees better with 'Defiance' trumpet blow.' Cf. also beaten, l. 6. 'Threate, threat' of 2 qu. is better with its wn readings, and 'Threaten' with its context.

⁷ '*snow*'=skin: therefore 'odour'd' is better than 'shining' of 2 qu. ⁸ '*so*' 2 qu. drop out in error.

⁹ Our text more expressive than 2 qu., 'there thou dost'=thou dost most oppress my most faith that is greater than that of any other. ¹ '*euils*'—as usual='ills.' So xii. l. 6 and xiv. l. 2.

VIII. Yet worse then worst,[2] I say thou art a theefe—
   A theefe !
   Now God forbid ! a theefe ! and of worst theeues
      the cheefe :[3]
   Theeues steal for need, and steale but[4] goods
      which paine recouers,
   But thou, rich in all ioyes,[5] dost rob my ioyes from
      me,
   Which cannot be restor'd by time or industrie :
   Of foes the spoyle[6] is euill, far worse of constant
      louers.

IX. Yet—gentle English theeues do rob, but will not
      slay,
   Thou English murdring theefe, wilt haue harts
      for thy prey : pray

---

[2] '*worst*': 2 qu. misprint 'worse.'

[3] '*cheefe*': 2 qu. misprint 'a thief.'

[4] '*but*': 2 qu. misprint 'for.'

[5] '*ioyes*': 2 qu. misprint 'goods'—for the strength of the accusation is that thieves steal 'goods' that can be recovered, but that she, rich in 'ioyes,' steals his 'ioyes.'

[6] '*spoyle*,' Q 1 and A and A 1613 : 'spoyles' of Q 2 takes its 's' from 'is,' and that verb shows the plural is wrong. 'Worse' is stronger, and agrees better with 'evil' than 'more,' 2 qu.

The name of murdrer now on thy faire forehead
    sitteth,
And euen while I do speake, my death-wounds
    bleeding be,
Which, I protest, proceed from only cruell thee :
Who may, and will not saue, murder in truth
    committeth.

x. But murder,[7] priuate fault, seemes but a toy to
    thee :
I lay then to thy charge vniustest[8] tyrannie,
If rule, by force, without all claim, a tyran show-
    eth ;
For thou dost lord my heart,[9] who am not borne
    · thy slaue,
And, which is worse, makes me, most guiltlesse,
    torments haue :
A rightfull prince by unright[1] deeds a tyran grow-
    eth.

---

[7] '*murder*' (collectively used) is proved to be right both by
'fault' and ' seemes ': 2 qu. have ' murthers.'
[8] '*unjustest*' : 2 qu. misprint 'injustice.'
[9] '*dost lord my heart*' is much more expressive of usurped
tyranny than 'for thou art my heart's lord.'
[1] '*unright*': 2 qu. ' unrightful '—former sharper, more cutting,
and fuller.

XI. Lo, you grow proud with this, for tyrans make
    folke bow:
Of foule rebellion then I do appeach thee now,
Rebell by Nature's law, rebell by law of Reason:
Thou, sweetest subiect wert, borne in the realme
    of Loue,
And yet against thy prince thy force dost daily
    proue:
No vertue merits praise, once toucht with blot of
    treason.

XII. But valiant rebels oft in fooles' mouths purchase
    fame:
I now then staine thy white with vagabonding[2]
    shame,
Both rebell to the sonne and vagrant from the
    mother;
For wearing Venus' badge in euery part of thee,
Vnto Dianae's traine thou, runnaway, didst flie:
Who faileth one is false, though trusty to another.

---

[2] '*vagabonding*': 2 qu. 'blackest blot of'—the latter tempting; but it is too strong, seeing that he blackens her more and more in each succeeding stanza. Here he merely blots any white she might have as a valiant rebel by proving her a vagabond also.

XIII. What, is not this enough ! nay, farre worse commeth here;
A witch, I say, thou art, though thou so faire appeare;
For, I protest, my sight[3] neuer thy face enioyeth,
But I in me am chang'd, I am aliue and dead,
My feete are turn'd to rootes, my hart becommeth lead :
No witchcraft is so euill as which man's mind destroyeth.

XIV. Yet witches may repent; thou art farre worse then they :
Alas that I am forst such euill of thee to say :
I say thou art a diuell, though cloth'd in angel's shining ;
For thy face tempts my soule to leaue the heav'n for thee,

---

[3] '*my sight* . . . . . *face*' : 2 qu. 'mine eyes . . . . . sight,' was probably altered, as in A and A 1613, because 'eyes' are plural, and the rhyming 'enjoyeth' singular.

And thy words of refuse do powre euen hell on
    mee :
Who tempt, and tempting plague, are diuels in
    true defining.[4]

xv. You, then, vngrateful theefe, you murdring tyran,
    you,
You rebell runaway, to lord and lady vntrue,
You witch, you diuell, alas, you still of me be-
    loued,
You see what I can say ; mend yet your froward
    mind,
And such skill in my Muse, you, reconcil'd, shall
    find,
That all these cruell words your praises shalbe
    proued.

---

[4] The construction is [those] who .... are : therefore 'tempt'
and 'plague' (A and A 1613), not 'tempts .... plagues' : l. 6,
2 qu. 'by' for 'all.'

SIXT SONG.

I. O YOU that heare this voice,
   O you that see this face,
   Say whether⁵ of the choice
   Deserues the former place :
   Feare not to iudge this bate,⁶
   For it is void of hate.

II. This side doth⁷ Beauty take,
    For that doth Musike speake ;
    Fit oratours to make
    The strongest iudgements weake :
    The barre to plead their⁸ right
    Is only true delight.

---

⁵ Cf. stanza ix. l. 5, in both 'whether'=which of the two.

⁶ '*bate*'=contention. See Glossarial Index, *s.v.* Query=our '*de-bate*'?

⁷ All the editions have 'doth' with a nominative which being double is plural, but where there is only one on each side, and the action of each separate.

⁸ '*their*': not 'the,' as in 2 qu. Both could not plead '*the* right.' The construction is, Only-true delight is the bar at which they plead, or rather where each pleads his right.

III. Thus doth the voice and face,
These gentle lawyers, wage,
Like louing brothers' case,
For father's heritage ;
That each, while each contends,
It selfe to other lends.

IV. For Beautie beautifies
With heauenly hew⁹ and grace
The heauenly harmonies ;
And in this faultlesse face
The perfect beauties be
A perfect harmony.

V. Musick more loftly¹ swels
In speeches nobly placed ;
Beauty as farre excels,
In action² aptly graced :
A friend each party draws
To countenance his cause.

---

⁹ ' *hew* ': 2 qu. misprint ' view.'

¹ ' *loftly* ': 2 qu. ' lustie '—a misplaced epithet, albeit its meaning has much changed since.

² ' *action* ': more idiomatic and technical than ' actions.' Hence

VI. Loue more affected seemes
To Beautie's louely light ;
And Wonder more esteemes
Of Musicke's wondrous might ;
But both to both so bent,
As both in both are spent.

VII. Musicke doth witnesse call
The eare his truth to trie ;
Beauty brings to the hall
Eye-iudgement[3] of the eye :
Both in their obiects such,
As no exceptions tutch.

VIII. The common sense, which might
Be arbiter of this,
To be, forsooth, vpright,
To both sides partiall is ;
He layes on this chiefe praise,
Chiefe praise on that he laies.

in i. l. 4, 'former' (A and A 1613) = the first of two, is probably the later, as it is superior to 'better' of 2 qu.

[3] '*Eye-iudgement*' (A and A 1613) = the special or 'expert' judgment of that organ : far more vivid than 'The judgement' of 2 qu.

IX. Then Reason, princesse hy,—
Whose throne is in the minde,
Which Musicke can in sky
And hidden beauties finde,—
Say whether thou wilt crowne
With limitlesse renowne?

SEUENTH SONG.

1. WHOSE senses in so euill consort[3] their step-
dame Nature laies,
That rauishing delight in them most sweete tunes
do[4] not raise;
Or if they do delight therein, yet are so closde[5]
with wit,

---

[3] '*consort*,' A and A 1613, as against 'comfort' (2 qu.) is proved by 'tunes' and l. 2 generally, and by the accentuation.

[4] '*do*,' A and A 1613, not 'doth' (2 qu.). The nominative is 'tunes,' and 'delight' is the accusative.

[5] '*closde*,' A and A 1613: the 2 qu. have 'cloi'd.' The former is preferable, for he does not mean to represent them as having a superabundance of wit, but only as 'closed up' in their own appreciation of their wit, and closed up against the delight they would otherwise welcome and enjoy. This is borne out by l. 4. Here 'it' might, at first sight, be supposed to refer to 'wit'; but

As with sententious lips to set a title⁶ vaine on it;
O let them heare these sacred tunes, and learne
    in Wonder's scholes,
To be, in things past bounds of wit, fooles—if they
    be not fooles.

11. Who haue so leaden eyes, as not to see sweet Beau-
    tie's show,
Or, seeing, haue so wooden⁷ wits, as not that worth
    to know,
Or, knowing, haue so muddy minds, as not to be in
    loue,

'a title vain' is the epithet they give, expressive of their view of its foolishness, that is, of the foolishness of the delight, or of the music that caused the delight. I say 'music,' because the intermediate 'therein' seems to have led Sidney to refer to sweet tunes, or rather to the main thought—the music contained in them—by a pronoun in the singular. Such ideal, rather than grammatical, concord was not uncommon in Elizabethan writings, and is not uncommon in conversation at the present day.

⁶ '*title*': 2 qu. stupidly misprint 'little.'
⁷ '*wooden*' = foolish.

Or, louing, haue so frothy thoughts,[8] as eas'ly thence
to moue;
O let them see these heauenly beames, and in faire letters reede
A lesson fit, both sight and skill, loue and firme loue to breede.

III. Heare then, but then with wonder heare, see, but adoring,[9] see,
No mortall gifts, no earthly fruites, now here descended[1] be':

---

[8] '*thoughts*,' A and A 1613 : 2 qu. 'hearts.' The latter seems to agree better with 'loving,' but 'thoughts' agrees better with 'frothy,' and this was a phrase frequently used a little later, as in Marston's Satires, &c. It will also be noted, that in the three lines all is referred to the intellect—'wooden wits'—'muddie minds'—'frothie thoughts.' In 'eas'ly,' A and A 1613, and 'easie' (2 qu.), the reading is indifferent.

[9] '*adoring*,' A and A 1613, is stronger, and agrees better with following lines, than 'admiring' (2 qu.); l. 4, 'life-giuing,' A and A 1613. The 2 qu., in error, read 'life-given '=the sun and moon, whose beams were life-giving in old philosophy.

[1] '*descended*,' A and A 1613 : 'discerned ' (2 qu.). Each may be a mistake for the other; but as both give sense, probably they are Author's variants. No gifts such as are given to mere

See, doo you see this face? a face, nay, image of
the skies,
Of which, the two life-giuing lights are figured in
her eyes :
Heare you this soule-inuading voice, and count it
but a voice ?
The very essence of their tunes, when angels do
rejoyce.

EIGHT SONG.[2]

1. IN a groue most rich of shade,
Where birds wanton musicke made,

---

mortals, no merely earthly fruits, are to be viewed here or
'discerned,' or have here 'descended' from the heavens.

[2] It may be that the additional verses in A and A 1613 editions
(stanzas xviii. xxvi.) of the present and Song x. were, from motives
of delicacy, not included in the copies (MS.) given by Sidney to
others than his intimates: and this is supported by the absence
previous to A of Sonnet xxxvii., the plainest of those in which the
name of Rich is introduced. While therefore, as against this
must be set the strangeness that these additional stanzas must
have been first 'divulged' in an edition published and edited, so
far at least as the Arcadia is concerned, by the Countess of Pem-

May, then yong, his pide weedes showing,
New-perfumed with flowers fresh growing : ³

II. Astrophel with Stella sweet
Did for mutual comfort meete,
Both within themselues oppressèd,
But each in the⁴ other blessèd.

III. Him great harmes had taught much care,
Her faire necke a foule yoke bare ;
But her sight his cares did banish,
In his sight her yoke did vanish :

broke, I do not insist on the argument that these additions betoken later versions. As in the others, however, the internal evidence in Song viii. proves this. The 2 qu. give one correction, 'woe' for 'woes' (v. l. 2).

³ May is not so much growing new perfumes, since they were the same year by year, as he is newly perfumed with the newly-opened flowers. Nor is he intended to be represented as a perfume-plant grower for Rimmel, as a youth garlanded with flowers, and newly-perfumed thereby. Hence A and A 1613 is the better, new-perfumed, and (,) removed, as in A 1613.

⁴ The metre being—˘ 'in the' (A and A 1613) is more rhythmical than 'in each' (2 qu.), besides being rather more correct.

IV. Wept they had, alas, the while,
    But now teares themselues did smile,
    While their eyes, by Loue directed;
    Enterchangeably reflected.

V. Sigh they did; but now betwixt
    Sighes of woe[5] were glad sighes mixt;
    With arms crost, yet testifying
    Restlesse rest, and liuing dying.

VI. Their eares hungrie of each word
    Which the deare tongue would afford;
    But their tongues restrain'd from walking,
    Till their harts had ended talking.

VII. But when their tongues could not speake,
     Loue it selfe did silence breake;
     Loue did set his lips asunder,
     Thus to speake in loue and wonder.

---

[5] '*Woes*,' A and A 1613, is probably an error for 'woe,' (2 qu.) through influence of 'sighs.' But in v. l. 1, 'sigh they did' is a subtle after-change from 'sigh'd they had ' (2 qu:), and far more descriptive. As they 'had wept' (stanza iv.), they had of course

VIII. Stella, soueraigne of my ioy,
　　　Faire triumpher⁶ of annoy;
　　　Stella, starre of heauenly fier,
　　　Stella, loadstar of desier;

IX. Stella, in whose shining eyes
　　　Are the lights of Cupid's skies,
　　　Whose beames, where they once are⁷ darted,
　　　Loue therewith is streight imparted;

X. Stella, whose voice, when it speakes,
　　　Senses all asunder breakes;
　　　Stella, whose voice, when it singeth,
　　　Angels to acquaintance bringeth;

sighed; now still he says they sighed, even in the joy of their meetings, but their sighs of grief at Fortune, their foe, were mingled with sighs of gladness.

⁶ '*Triumphres*' (2 qu.) has an uncouth sound, and if invented by Sidney, was probably on after-thought discarded: 'in' (2 qu.) cannot be right; the 'annoy' is his 'annoy.' 'Of'=off or from, is, on the other hand, admissible.

⁷ '¯*Once ăre*,' A and A 1613, better than 'āre ōnce' (2 qu.).

XI. Stella, in whose body is
Writ each caracter[8] of blisse;
Whose face all, all beauty[9] passeth,
Saue thy mind, which it[1] surpasseth.

XII. Graunt, O graunt; but speach, alas,
Failes me, fearing on to passe :
Graunt,[2] O me : what am I saying?
But no fault there is in praying.

XIII. Graunt—O deere, on knees I pray,
(Knees on ground he then did stay)
That, not I, but since I loue[3] you,
Time and place for me may[4] moue you.

---

[8] '*each character*,' A and A 1613, more expressive than 'the characters' (2 qu.).

[9] '*sweete*,' 2 qu.: an insufficient and poor epithet, when one speaks of all-surpassing loveliness.

[1] '*thy* .... *it*,' A and A 1613 : 'the' (2 qu.) is almost without doubt an error for 'thy'; and though 'yet' (2 qu.) gives sense, our text is by each of the changes made the clearer.

[2] '*graunt—O me*,' A and A 1613. This third repetition of 'grant,' without ability to proceed, is far more expressive than 'to me' (2 qu.) : 'fault' (*ib.*) is more fitting than 'sin' (2 qu.).

[3] '*proue*,' 2 qu.: no sense with 'and.'

[4] '*nere*,' 2 qu. : reverses Sidney's meaning.

xiv. Neuer season was more fit;
   Neuer roome more apt for it;
   Smiling ayre allowes my reason;
   These birds sing, ' Now vse the season.'

xv. This small wind, which so sweete is,
   See how it the leaues doth kisse;
   Each tree in his best attiring,
   Sense of loue to loue inspiring.

xvi. Loue makes earth the water drink,
   Loue to earth makes water sinke;
   And, if dumbe things be so witty,
   Shall a heauenly grace want pitty?

xvii. There his hands, in their speech, faine
   Would haue made tongue's language plaine;
   But her hands, his hands repelling,[5]
   Gaue repulse all grace excelling.[6]

---

[5] '*repelling*,' A and A 1613: 2 qu. 'compelling'—bad.

[6] Her after-words do not admit of 'expelling' (2 qu.): and 'excelling,' A and A 1613, is the far better description, and one which agrees with other sayings of Sidney regarding her. Her

XVIII. Then she spake ; her speech was such,
So⁷ not eares, but hart did tuch :   heart
While such-wise she loue denièd,
And yet loue she signifièd.

XIX. Astrophel, sayd she, my loue,
Cease, in these effects, to proue ;
Now be still, yet still beleeue me,
Thy griefe more then death would grieue me.

XX. If that any thought in me
Can tast comfort but of thee,
Let me, fed with hellish anguish,
Ioylesse, hopelesse, endlesse languish.

XXI. If those eyes you praisèd, be
Halfe so deare as you to me,
Let me home returne, starke blinded
Of those eyes, and blinder minded ;

---

refusal was a grace, her repulse a movement excelling àll grace in its very denial.

⁷ ' *So*,' A and A 1613 : evidently a change from ' with ' (2 qu.) and for the better.

XXII. If to secret of my hart,
    I do any wish impart,
    Where thou art not formost placèd,
    Be both wish and I defacèd.

XXIII. If more may be sayd, I say,
    All my blisse in thee I lay;
    If thou loue, my loue, content thee,
    For all loue, all faith is meant thee.

XXIV. Trust me, while I thee deny,
    In my selfe the smart I try;
    Tyran Honour doth thus vse thee,
    Stella's selfe might not refuse thee.

XXV. Therefore, deare, this no more moue,
    Least, though I leaue not thy loue,
    Which too deep in me is framèd,
    I should blush when thou art namèd.

XXVI. Therewithall away she went,
    Leauing him to passion rent,
    With what she had done and spoken,
    That therewith my song is broken.

NINTH SONG.

I. GO, my flocke, go, get you hence,
    Seeke a better place of feeding,
    Where you may haue some defence
    Fro[8] the stormes in my breast breeding,
    And showers from mine eyes proceeding.

II. Leaue a wretch, in whom all wo
    Can abide to keepe no measure;
    Merry flock, such one forego,
    Vnto whom mirth is displeasure,
    Onely rich in mischief's[9] treasure.

III. Yet, alas, before you go,
    Heare your wofull maister's story,
    Which to stones I els would show:
    Sorrow only then hath glory
    When 'tis excellently sorry.

---

[8] '*Fro*,' A and A 1613: 'For' a modern error.
[9] '*mischief's*': 2 qu. 'measure's'—error.

IV. Stella, fiercest shepherdesse,
 Fiercest, but yet fairest euer ;[1]
 Stella, whom, O heauens still blesse,
 Though against me she perseuer,
 Though I blisse enherit neuer :

V. Stella hath refusèd me !
 Stella, who more loue hath prouèd,
 In this caitife heart to be,
 Then can in good eawes[2] be mouèd   ewes
 Toward lambkins best belouèd.

VI. Stella hath refusèd me !
 Astrophel, that so well seruèd
 In this pleasant Spring must see,[3]

---

[1] In 2 qu. l. 1, 'fairest' for 'fiercest'; l. 2, 'fairest' for 'fiercest,' and 'cruelst' for 'fairest' of A and A 1613. The changes in A and A 1613 accord better with l. 3, as well as his supposed thoughts. So l. 3, 'O' (A and A 1613) for 'the' (2 qu.) ; but though 'do' is shown by these changes to be later, it may be questioned whether, to our ears, it sounds as well as 'still,' 2 qu.

[2] 'to us,' 2 qu. : a strange meaningless error for 'ewes' (A and A 1613).

[3] To make sense out of Muse, 2 qu., a (.) has been placed

While in pride flowers be preseruèd,
Himselfe onely Winter-steruèd.

VII. Why, alas, doth she then sweare [4]
That she loueth me so dearely,
Seeing me so long to beare
Coles of loue that burne so cleerly,
And yet leaue me helplesse meerely?

VIII. Is that loue? forsooth, I trow,
If I saw my good dog grieuèd,
And a helpe for him did know,
My loue should not be beleeuèd,
But he were by me releeuèd.

---

after 'served,' but he is talking to his flock,—not to his Muse, who has no business there. I read 'must,' A and A 1613, and re-punctuate.

[4] I prefer rhythm of A and A 1613, and in l. 5, 'helpless' for 'hopeless' (2 qu.). He could not be said to be 'hopeless': cf. ll. 1-2,—but he says, if she love as she says, why does she leave me without relief? These are sufficient to prove A and A 1613 later and better; and hence I adopt their readings in stanzas ix. and x. against 2 qu.—viz. ix. l. 3, 'Knowing if she should dis-play'; x. l. 1, 'my dear flocke now.' In ix. l. 4, 'her' (A and A 1613) is required by the metre, and is erroneously omitted in 2 qu.

ix. No, she hates me, well-away,
   Faining loue, somewhat to please me ;
   For she knows, if she display
   All her hate, death soone would seaze me,
   And of hideous torments ease me.

x. Then adieu, deare flocke, adieu ;
   But, alas, if in your straying
   Heauenly Stella meete with you,
   Tell her, in your pitious blaying,
   Her poore slaue's uniust decaying.

TENTH SONG.

1. O DEARE life, when shall it be
   That mine eyes thine eyes shall[5] see,
   And in them thy mind discouer
   Whether absence haue had force
   Thy remembrance to diuorce
   From the image of thy louer?

---

[5] I prefer 'shall' (A), both because of 'shall' above, and because it is more expressive of present deprivation than 'may.'

II. Or if I my self find not,
   After parting, aught⁶ forgot,
   Nor debar'd from Beautie's treasure,
   Let not tongue aspire to tell
   In what high ioyes I shall dwell;
   Only thought aymes at the pleasure.

III. Thought, therefore, I will send thee
   To take vp the place for me:
   Long I will not after tary,
   There, vnseene, thou mayst be bold,
   Those faire wonders to behold,
   Which in them my hopes do cary.

IV. Thought, see thou no place forbeare,
   Enter brauely euerywhere,
   Seize on all to her belonging;
   But if thou wouldst garded be,
   Fearing her beames, take with thee
   Strength of liking, rage of longing.

---

⁶ '*aught*,' A and A 1613; 'oft' (2 qu.)—former far better. As to the rest, 'after parting' (A and A 1613) is clearer, though not so expressive of her having left him, as 'By thine absence oft forgot'; but I adopt the former. See note on Sonnet lxxxvii.

v. Thinke of that most gratefull time
   When my⁷ leaping heart will climb,
   In thy lips to haue his biding,
   There those roses for to kisse,
   Which do breathe a sugred blisse,
   Opening rubies, pearles dividing.

vi. Thinke of my most princely power,
    Which I blessèd shall devower
    With my greedy licorous sences,
    Beauty, musicke, sweetnesse, loue,
    While she doth against me proue
    Her strong darts but weake defences.

vii. Thinke, thinke of those dalyings,
     When with doue-like murmurings,
     With glad moning,⁸ passèd anguish,
     We change eyes, and hart for hart,   heart
     Each to other do depart,
     Ioying till ioy makes vs languish.

⁷ '*my*,' A 1613: 2 qu. and all seemingly, oddly misprint 'thy.'
⁸ '*moning passèd*,' the sense being anguish [being] passèd;
l. 5, 'depart'=part with. See note on Sonnet lxxxvii.

VIII. O my thought,⁹ my thoughts surcease,
Thy delights my woes increase,
My life melts¹ with too much thinking;
Thinke no more, but die in me,
Till thou shalt reuiuèd be,
At her lips my nectar drinking.

ELEUENTH SONG.²

1. 'WHO is it that this darke night
    Vnderneath my window playneth?'
It is one who from thy sight
Being, ah, exil'd, disdayneth
Euery other vulgar light.

11. 'Why, alas, and are you he?
. Be not yet those fancies changèd?'
Deare, when you find change in me,

---

⁹ '*thought*,' A and A 1613, as a being that has thoughts—his intellectual part. Cf. stanzas ii. l. 5, iii. l. 1, iv. l. 1, and v. l. 1, vi. l. 1, vii. l. 1.   ¹ '*melts*': 2 qu. 'fleetes.'

² This first appeared in A 1598; A 1613 has two gross errors, viz. st. viii. l. 5, 'thee' for 'there,' as in 1598 and 1605. In the Bright MS. 'there' correctly.

Though from me you be estrangèd,
Let my chaunge to ruine be.

III. 'Well, in absence this will dy;
Leaue to see, and leaue to wonder.'
Absence sure will helpe, if I
Can learne how my selfe to sunder
From what in my hart doth ly.

IV. 'But time will these thoughts remoue;
Time doth work what no man knoweth.'
Time doth as the subiect proue;
With time still the affection groweth
In the faithful turtle-doue.

V. 'What if we new beauties see,
Will not they stir new affection?'
I will thinke they pictures be,
(Image-like, of saints' perfection)
Poorely counterfeting thee.

VI. 'But your reason's purest light
Bids you leaue such minds to nourish.'
Deere, do reason no such spite;
Neuer doth thy beauty florish
More then in my reason's sight.

VII. 'But the wrongs Loue beares will make
   Loue at length leaue undertaking.'
   No, the more fooles it doth shake,
   In a ground of so firme making
   Deeper still they driue the stake.

VIII. 'Peace, I thinke that some giue eare;
   Come no more, least I get anger.'
   Blisse, I will my blisse forbeare;
   Fearing, sweete, you to endanger;
   But my soule shall harbour there.

IX. 'Well, be gone; be gone, I say,
   Lest that Argus' eyes perceiue you.'
   O vniust[3] is Fortune's sway,
   Which can make me thus to leaue you;
   And from lowts[4] to run away.

---

[3] '*uniust*,' A and A 1605 and 1613: 'unjust is,' later A: 'unjustest,' Bright MS.

[4] '*lowts*' = obeisances. See Glossarial Index. G.

END OF VOL. I.

ROBERT ROBERTS, PRINTER, BOSTON, LINCOLNSHIRE.

www.ingramcontent.com/pod-product-compliance
Lightning Source LLC
Chambersburg PA
CBHW032118230426
43672CB00009B/1784